How to Start a Successful Business - The First Time

The Definitive Business Startup Guide from Concept through Financing and Operating Your Business - The Right Way!

By

Gary C. Bizzo

To Nick My friend & Mentor Biz 2014

BizPak One
One of a Series

Gary C. Bizzo
APEC, Certified Business Counselor
Vancouver
2013

Table of Contents

HOW TO START A SUCCESSFUL BUSINESS - THE FIRST TIME

Chapter One   **1**

What Keeps Entrepreneurs Awake at Night?   **1**

Overview of a Start-up   3
The Entrepreneur Tipping Point   6
What Makes an Entrepreneur Successful?   7
Traits of a Successful Entrepreneur   9

Chapter Two   **11**

Challenges Entrepreneurs Face   **11**

Hello Entrepreneur   11
Passion & Timing   13
Things to Consider Before You Quit Your Job   15

Chapter Three   **19**

One Idea, One Business   **19**

Startup or Buy an Existing Business?   19
Working on Your Business Not In It   23
Focus   28
Naming Your Business   28
Seven Tagline (slogan) Ideas for Your Business   32
Basing Business on Solutions to a Problem   33

Chapter Four   **35**

The Nuts & Bolts   **35**

What Makes a Great Business Plan?   35
The Business Plan Essentials   38
What Form of Business Will You Have?   42
Your Unique Selling Proposition or Point (USP)   43
Location, Location, Location, What Entrepreneurs Need to Know   44

The Elevator Pitch   46

Chapter Five   48

Finance - Show Me the MONEY   48
Financial & Business Goals   48
Financing your Business   50

Chapter Six   54

Marketing – The Art of Customer Acquisition   54
Marketing, Service, Quality   54
Revenue Streams   54
Guerrilla Marketing Increases Business   56
SWOT Analysis   60
Finding a Niche   61
Corporate Intelligence   62
Types of Marketing from Viral to Engagement   67
Strategic Alliances.   72
Tips on Direct Marketing   73

Chapter Seven   76

Engaging Your Clients   76
Social Media Marketing, the New Standard   76
Engagement Marketing & Social Media Networking   78
Inbound vs. Outbound Marketing   79
Raise Your Game, Entrepreneurs – Social Media/Inbound Marketing   81
Comparing Social Media   82
Social Media Reputation Management   84

Chapter Eight   86

No Sales No Business   86
Pricing Your Product or Service   87
Sales Funnel   89
80/20 Rule   90
Customer Service   90

Chapter Nine   **95**

Managing What You've Got   **95**
Business Management   95
Building Your Dream Team for Your Business   96
Networking   99
Successful Business Networking   102

Chapter Ten   **104**

Finding the Entrepreneur Within   **104**
Develop Your Confidence   104
Doubt Kills the Warrior   104
Success Fuels the Warrior   105
Achievement   106
Ask for Help   107
Mentors   109
Mentoring Others   110

Chapter Eleven   **114**

New Methods or Ways to Do Business   **114**
Eight Tips for the Budding Entrepreneur   114
The Healer vs. the Corporate Wellness Coach   116
How to Keep Yourself Happy in Your Own Business   117

Chapter Twelve   **120**

Some Other Considerations   **120**
The Business Startup   120
Women Make Better Entrepreneurs!   121
The Reluctant Entrepreneur   124
Franchise Businesses   126
Rebranding a Company or Product   128
Alternative Corporations- An Overview of Social Enterprises,
Societies & Charities   130
Separating Home & Business   133

Chapter Thirteen 135

You've Made It or Not! Now What? 135
Making It or Not 135
Pay It Backward CEO's 137
What if You Can't Make It as an Entrepreneur - the Intrapreneur 138

Chapter Fourteen 140

The Big Exit 140
Exit Strategies 140
Five Reasons Someone Would Want to Acquire Your Company 141

Chapter Fifteen 144

Give me an Entrepreneur with Heart, Commitment 144
Pondering Changing Roles 146

Appendices 148
Social Media Checklist - How to Be A Social Media Rock Star 149
Self-Employment Assessment Test 158
Business Planning Worksheet 160
Biz Check List 165
Business Name Brainstorming 167
Business Plan Structure – Start Up Operations 168
Market Research Action Plan 171
Permits and Licensing Action Plan 172
Action Plan – Are You Ready & Organized Enough? 173
Action Plan - Hello Entrepreneur 175
Action Plan - Strategic Alliances 176
Action Plan – Unique Selling Point (USP) 177
The Marketing Plan – An Outline 178
Building Your Brand 180

Case Studies 182
Startup, Retail Mobile Flower Shop 182
Startup, Environmental Technologies/Project Management 190
Startup, Change Management – Graphic Business 198

Startup, R&D, Invention Development   204
Growth, Marketing Land Development Corp   209
Startup, B2B, Food & Beverage   216
Growth, Service Industry   221
Startup, Distribution Hospitality   227
Startup, Health Industry   233
Growth, Service Industry   238

BizPublishing:Publisher

Cover Design: Jonathan Moran

Production & Composition: Jo Ann Bizzo
Editing: Helmi BM (Australia)

This publication is designed to provide accurate and authoritative information in regard to the subject matter covered. It is sold with the understanding that the publisher is not engaged in rendering legal, accounting or other professional services. If legal advice or other expert assistance is required, the services of a competent professional person should be sought.

Library of Congress Cataloging-in-Publication Data

Bizzo, Gary Clifford.

How to Start a Successful Business – the First Time: The Definitive Business Startup Guide from Concept through Financing to Operating Your Business, the Right Way! / By Gary C. Bizzo

ISBN 978-0-9920988-0-3 Paper

ISBN 978-0-9920988-1-0 Digital PDF

1. Startup. 2. Entrepreneur. 3. Business.

Acknowledgements

I have amazing people in my life who have given me inspiration in this project and support when needed.

My clients mean a great deal to me and I hope they feel they have gotten the best advice over the years. They have given me great joy by working with them.

Thank you to a dear friend and colleague, **Carl de Jong**. I joined an entrepreneurial program Carl taught more than twenty years ago when I was a commercial photographer. His program and subsequent introduction to Michael Gerber was the basis for where I am today.

My inspiration over the years has been other authors who I respect specifically **Jack Whyte**, author of the *The Camulod Chronicles,* www.camulod.com. Jack showed me the passion in writing. **Rick Dennis**, a very old friend and broadcaster/writer who should have written for Rolling Stone Magazine. With the in-depth articles he wrote based on interviews with famous musicians he always gave you insight into them that you never would have gotten anywhere else. His reviews and interviews could never be surpassed.

Michael Gerber, author of the EMyth and considered the #1 Business Coach in the world, inspired my business life with his "working on your business not in it" philosophy. I've had the pleasure of working with him. Michael is an inspiration.

A fellow Author, **Nick Noorani**, is my mentor and a future collaborator. Thanks Nick!

I want to thank my many reviewers, mostly friends and family who came to my rescue, including Mary Lynn & Shawn Cunningham, Amanda Arnold, Gerardo Ernesto, Banjo Benjamin, Dave Stephen and Kathy Maccallum.

Special thanks to my wife, Jo Ann, who always believes in me. She is a constant support.

Dedication

To the entrepreneurs of the world both in body and mind who know there is another destiny in their life besides a 9-5 job – those who go for it!

To my wife, Jo Ann, your unconditional love gives me everything and it goes both ways, love ya baby!

Gary C. Bizzo has 30 years experience in fulfilling the needs of business. He was a Commercial Photographer with an international reputation, Marketing/Business Consultant and is an Agent of Change on Social Media. His boutique advertising agency provided custom services to a wide variety of businesses. He has been a Mentor and/or Business Coach to 1000+ Vancouver based businesses and consults with numerous multinationals. He also writes Business articles local, regional and national magazines.

Introduction

I wanted to write a book that would allow new entrepreneurs ease of entry into the business world. What I found out was that it wasn't just for the young twenty something kid right out of school.

I was writing for the man tired of working 14 hours a day by himself in a dead-end job with no respite, for the woman who came to me telling me she had six different businesses opened and closed within seven years and the 65 year old baby boomer wanting to supplement a meager pension who had an 'idea'.

I wanted to help the 50 year old man who had ulcers because of the 30 year old boss who was bullying him to leave his job and the single mother who had that great art craft idea for kids only a mother could conjure up.

I've counseled a client who loved people and who always wanted to open a coffee shop but had nagging doubt followed by another client who hated people but thought a coffee shop was a money maker. Then there was the young woman with lofty ideas who wanted to start an airline - she did. Some succeed but most are left at the curb with little to show but debt.

This book is for those with a passion and a spirit who just need a little help.

Chapter One

What Keeps Entrepreneurs Awake at Night?

Having been an entrepreneur for over 30 years, a young reporter asked me to comment on "What Keeps Entrepreneurs Awake at Night." That question resonated deep within me because I knew the answer firsthand.

As a young entrepreneur, a fine, and not so fine, scotch put me to sleep many nights when faced with what appeared to be insurmountable problems.

The primary thing that I have learned over the years is that we fail to get past the Technician role in our businesses. According to Michael Gerber, author of the E-Myth, there are 3 people in the head of each business owner; the Technician, the Manager and the Entrepreneur. There exists a distinct difference and process as each of us grows through those roles and levels in our businesses.

Once an entrepreneur can give away control of doing the work, of the technician, and move onto the manager role, the stress will diminish and that increasing workload will take a different turn. Now your goal is to keep your new employees busy and get out of your head that confused notion that you gave away control - that only you can do the job right. Once you can break this barrier you have taken the first step to being the entrepreneur you hoped was within you.

I asked a client who owned a one man computer repair shop when he thought he might be over the 'hump' in his business. He thought for a minute and said that in year five he thinks he might be able to take a week holiday to his home country with his wife. He didn't get the concept of Technician and how the only way to be free was to replace him in the day to day operation of the business.

Organization will give you a good night's sleep. Planning on a regular basis and time management seems to elude the average business person. I used to get up in the middle of the night with worry and run to my computer to jot down some ideas, ahggh.

It took me years to understand the basic concept of time management and planning. It also doesn't help a marriage, or two.

Financial planning, or lack of, specifically, is critical. In the old days, working from home was a no-no; it made you look like an amateur. In keeping with that theory, I had, of course, a huge 5000 foot, turn of the century (1908), old bank as my office in downtown Vancouver. It had 26 foot ceilings, paneled office walls of mahogany and even a locking bank vault. They filmed the movie, *Mr. Magoo*, in my office.

Imagine trying to come up with that overhead each month; high-speed T1 Internet line $3000, rent $5000 plus, plus, plus. Now everyone has a home office if possible because it is acceptable to work from home.

When I talk to clients it seems having enough operating capital is always a problem. There's never enough planning in how much money an entrepreneur needs to setup their business primarily because no one considers doing a startup budget. It seems logical to me to have one. What do people say about common sense?

Prepaying for the pain is my favorite concept that keeps us awake at night. I remember doing a job for the Holiday Inn and had made my invoice. With a high five figure invoice even I was aghast, thinking that my client would be upset and question my billing. I ignored my client's calls for a week and could not sleep with worry. I finally made an appointment on Friday for the following Monday to present my bill. I didn't sleep all weekend.

On Monday I pulled my courage together, gave the CEO my invoice and waited for a tongue lashing at the very least. He thanked me for a job well done, reached in his desk drawer, pulled out his checkbook and wrote a check for $75,000. We went on to do a lot of business together, yikes! I had suffered for nothing. – My new mantra? *Doubt Kills the Warrior*. The corollary to that is *Success Fuels the Warrior*!

Deadlines? I've come to observe that contracts, deadlines and schedules must have guidelines. I've sweated over performance based deadlines many times. Once I explained the scenario to waiting clients it was easier to reevaluate and renegotiate time lines than to have a heart attack over missing one.

It all comes down to planning, financial management and understanding that you don't have to run your business all by yourself!

Overview of a Start-up

So you like to work around the backyard building lawn furniture which your friends tell you are absolutely amazing. They won't buy one of them, mind you, but the compliment is welcomed by you - another ego is stroked.

You think that perhaps there is some money out there in those hills if you open a business to sell this marvelous furniture. Fast forward a couple of weeks to new fancy business cards, a one page black and white flyer printed on cheap paper and maybe you've scored a website too. You're off to a good start except for a few things.

Have you started a business and registered the name? Have you even checked out if the name is available? I bet you did a Google search of the name and found nothing. It also means nothing because Google won't show up a registered business name unless it's active and/or used in a website.

What principles did you follow in the design of your business cards and flyer? Did you include a sales pitch or 'call to action' on the flyer or did you just give your name and a price (typically undervalued by 2 to 3 times of what you should be charging). You developed a marketing plan to determine where to best spend your startup money didn't you?

Startup money? I hope you have enough to put into your business. Consider enough for starting expenses plus 6 months of operating capital.

You have a well written plan and goals, correct?

What will be the type of company you setup, a corporation, sole proprietorship, partnership?

Are your family and friends on board with you? Unless they can support you with the time required and the other sacrifices, you may run into relationship issues. Oh, and don't borrow from your family.

How do you handle setbacks? When you are smiling, the whole company smiles with you.

Are you really an inventor, rather than an entrepreneur?

Can you accept that your company may outgrow you?

When you look in the mirror, does an entrepreneur look back?

We don't mean personal characteristics -- or not just personal characteristics, anyway. Do you believe you have all the skills, energy, money, people, and knowledge to start a business? Founders who carefully identify and evaluate their resources in pursuit of a well-defined goal display "entrepreneurial self-efficacy," a trait many academics believe to be the best predictor of success.

A founder may set out in a canoe, but pretty soon, he is sailing a yacht with investors and employees on board and their families huddled below deck. Risking your own fortunes is easy compared with risking the fortunes of those who believe in you. "These people may not completely understand the business," says J. Robert Baum, an associate professor of entrepreneurship at the University of Maryland. "They may not understand the level of risk. But they think they'll be OK because you are so smart. Breaking their dreams is very painful."

Do you have a mentor or someone to bounce ideas off?

Do you have a niche as the backyard handyman, e.g. on your new business card did you identify yourself as a lawn furniture builder or a handyman. You must stand out!

Do you have samples of your work? Best to work on that one.

Can you run your business from home or do you need office or work space?

Are you motivated enough to keep going when the going gets really tough? You must figure a way to keep motivated.

Will you know when it is time to close the business and move on? I have had several clients that won't close their businesses even if it clearly isn't working. They plod along expecting a miracle.

I had a client once who was a lawyer with an MBA – wow! I was surprised when he asked for help. He told me he needed to know the basics to run his law practice. I asked him what they taught him in law school and what his MBA taught him about business.

He laughed and said the MBA taught him about global economics, change management and a bunch of things that would help him if he was going to work for a corporate giant. He gave me a challenge to call his law school and ask them what tools they gave him to do business in the real world. I knew the answer but called anyway. The registrar of the law school laughed when I told him the dilemma. He reminded me that the law school was the pillar of the community and had been in existence several hundred years. Yes, "I know" I told him "but what do you teach them about business". The answer - "nothing, it's a law school after all not a business school."

Well, now I knew what I was up against, a man needing help with advanced degrees and little common sense to get him through life. I worked with him and it was a delight because he was used to working hard and listened carefully to everything I taught him. He has a very large successful law business today. I hope I will never need him.

Considering starting your own enterprise is a monumental undertaking and planning is the cornerstone of its success. You can get a basic Business Plan template from most banks and they will even help you fill it out. (See the Appendix for a sample)

The Entrepreneur Tipping Point

I was talking with my wife, Jo Ann, one night about being an entrepreneur. She's glad I have the entrepreneurial spirit but knows it isn't for the faint of heart and at the very least is a daunting challenge. Jo Ann is a woman with good ideas, an exceptionally strong work ethic (starting her working career as a pre-teen) and with a strong desire to get ahead, she is a natural to be an entrepreneur but... has doubt.

It's scary and certainly a slippery slope being an entrepreneur wannabe. Many entrepreneurs become one out of necessity, being laid off from a long held job usually from an economic downturn making a job redundant, an immigrant unable to find employment suitable to his qualifications, a youth out of university unable to find a job or a baby boomer being told he is too old.

Another entrepreneur develops from someone who has had it with an overzealous incompetent employer (this one fits my move to being an entrepreneur), a manager suffering from the Peter Principle (a manager who reaches his level of incompetence) and/or a system which doesn't give employees sufficient kudos, benefits and challenges to keep them as an employee.

This brings us to the employee/entrepreneur tipping point, the point at which we realize the benefits of self employment (can't believe I used that word instead of entrepreneur) outweighs the inconsistencies and hidden dangers of being an entrepreneur.

My wife pointed out that it is a difficult decision to quit a 'good' job with benefits. The benefits include pension plans, dental, structure, a place to fit in, and a place where you get recognition (well maybe that's a stretch).

After all is said and done I think that you can't decide to be an entrepreneur based on weighing the pros and cons. It's more like a gut feeling - mind you it might be a bellyache at times but clearly it's a choice one must make.

What Makes an Entrepreneur Successful?

Take 2 dashes of guts, basic business knowledge, a splash of common sense, access to financing and a smidgeon of luck and that is the recipe for a successful business.

Obviously that can be said of any endeavor. Success in Business is sometimes a fleeting thing. I see people with MBA's floundering in a new startup, lawyers doing poorly in practice and other professionals not reaching a level of achievement that is expected of them.

Do you have the education, skills and experience to pull this off? If you don't measure up, how can you compensate via volunteering, job shadowing, interning or hiring someone who really knows the business? Be sure to add this info in detail to your business plan.

There are self employment government funded programs in many Canadian cities providing skills that are both hard and soft in terms of knowledge base. Many governments in your jurisdiction have business agencies that provide workshops dealing with the nuts and bolts of operating a business while giving people insights and experiential knowledge that combines well with 'normal' business training in the strictest sense.

In the government funded self employment programs, basic accounting, financial, internet and web skills, marketing and sales skills that combined with insight and personal relevance are taught that make or break a business. I used to teach a workshop on how to name your company. Naming your company seems to be a relatively simple process but many find it daunting and forget to take into account Google or yellow page searches, phonetics, cultural misunderstandings of the name, spelling, etc.

Most small businesses need help with understanding the financial picture and health of their business. This includes knowing the amount of money needed to run the business for a minimum of 6 months and having financial backup in place from a bank, family or friends in case of a crunch. Knowing about financing need not take the place of the bookkeeper or accountant but you should know apples and oranges when talking to those professionals.

Marketing is of equal importance to proper financing. If you can't get your product or service out to the masses you will languish in your home office waiting for the phone to ring. You won't have any need for accounting services at that point.

In the entrepreneurial program I operated, we provided a great deal of mentoring and advisory services. I had a professional and certified business coach assigned to each new client-entrepreneur and that coach stayed with the client for a year while they were building their business. Specialty mentors came in as needed, e.g. a CGA may help a client with financing or accounting issues while a generalist mentor may be a retired photographer who could advise a photographer client in matters of overall photography business.

I also initiated small groups of entrepreneurs who joined together in teams of four as Peer Groups. The Peer Group met once a month and supported each other. After all, the only thing they really had in common was that they all were entrepreneurs in a startup mode.

We utilized networking where possible to have my clients (80 per year) meet other entrepreneurs to gain insights, knowledge and 'tricks' of their trade. We utilized in-house networking events, Boards of Trade receptions and events like www.meetup.com where groups advertised networking meetings.

People often refer to that successful entrepreneur as 'the self-made' man. That's like saying the Beatles was an overnight sensation. Some people luck into situations and some seemingly are always on top. Donald Trump has been bankrupt and lost hundred of millions but is seen as a major success and self-made man. I'd say one in a hundred people have the total combination of luck, drive, passion, money and other resources to be self-made.

The seemingly huge rise in entrepreneurism is not a Canadian phenomenon. In April 2009, soon after major layoffs occurred in Canada, Statistics Canada reported 9000 entrepreneurs started businesses in that month. Other countries followed suit. Self employment provides people who are sitting on the employment fence with motivation and transition to do 'what they always wanted to do' that is to setup their business.

In British Columbia, we have a lot of new immigrants who often have good business skills and business savvy, some financing in place but they lack not only the language skills but also the cultural sensibilities and nuances of conducting business in Canada. They need to try harder to succeed and know it. The single most cause for concern with new immigrant business people is the lack of integration and understanding of the culture. This culture can mean the buying habits of Canadians, demographics as well as understanding Canadian taste and language. My buddy, Nick Noorani, best-selling author and an immigrant himself, has written a good handbook for new immigrants called Arrival Survival, a must read for people trying to adapt and integrate into the Canadian culture.

The best way to become successful? It's called diligence and putting your passion to work!

Traits of a Successful Entrepreneur

You want an easy guide to be that successful business person you always wanted to become? Guess again, there is no panacea, no magic amulet (although inventing one might be your ticket) and nothing as easy as one, two and three. I've found that there are some traits entrepreneurs usually possess that are common in those who have found success.

Expert knowledge - you really must have the experience and a deep understanding of your product or service to sell yourself properly.

Strategic Vision – you must be driven to succeed in your business, living and breathing your dream.

Carpe Diem – You must be able to seize the opportunities and the moments given to you.

Networking – a good networker will not only look for opportunities for himself but keep an eye open for others; a good referral will always come back to you.

Extroverted - Unless you're running an Internet business with no accessibility to others or live in a cave you cannot be a loner in business. You must like people especially your customers.

Optimistic - If you tend to look at the glass half empty you will find it hard to have the necessary enthusiasm to excite others about your business.

Handle Stress - Let me tell you this is an important one. Being an entrepreneur is not for the faint of heart, you may need to be able to manage stress.

Persistence - Stick-to-it-ive-ness or what ever you call it. Brian Scudamore, CEO of 1-800-Got-Junk tried to obtain that memorable phone number which was already in use. He made 78 phone calls before someone said he could have it. Determination was the key.

Lifelong Learning - Learn from your mistakes as well as your victories. Successful entrepreneurs see business as a continuous learning experience with a lot of fine tuning of accepted practices and procedures.

Communication - You must be able to get your message out to your customers, as well as your employees.

Chapter Two

Challenges Entrepreneurs Face

Hello Entrepreneur

In April 2009, 9000 new businesses were started in British Columbia and 35,000 in Canada. (Financial Post)

It's hard to believe, but it also changed the face of the unemployment figures for the month, a figure which hadn't increased in several months.

Why? Well the unemployment figures represent people unemployed looking for employment. If you start a new business you are taken off the stats of the unemployed. Some consider Self Employment the last resort if you are out of work.

I think of it as the <u>opportunity of your lifetime</u>!

Yes Entrepreneurs, wear this label with pride! You have decided to take the risk to be your own boss; this is the opportunity to decide your own destiny; you will control your time and the time of those you employ. This is the chance to make a difference in your life so now you need to get serious about planning your business and asking those around you for advice.

Now that you have decided to be your own boss, I'd suggest you get a piece of paper and go talk to 3 entrepreneurs that you know. Ask them the following questions then compare them to the answers. They will be the same!

What was the biggest challenge they faced in starting up their business?

What types of unanticipated problems did they encounter?

What kind of support did they wish they had when they were starting out?

When did they feel they were 'over the hump'?

Did their vision of the business change at all over the course of the first year?

What would they do differently if they could do it over?

I want you to take this little questionnaire seriously. It may take only a few minutes over a coffee and doesn't have to be a formal meeting. Most people are attentive and appreciate being asked questions about how they succeeded. Your meeting might even give you a future alliance or a customer.

After you have interviewed those 3 entrepreneurs compare the answers (in italics) they gave you to the following other entrepreneurs have given me:

What was the biggest challenge in starting up their business?

Lack of planning.

Not enough capital.

Not having the right resources.

What type of problems did they encounter that they hadn't anticipated?

a)   *Financial.*

b)   *Seventy hour work weeks.*

c)   *HR and employees.*

What kind of support did they wish they had when they were starting out?

a)   *A mentor.*

b)   *A business plan.*

c)   *A friendly banker.*

When did they feel they were 'over the hump'?

a)   *Never.*

b)   *When I made my first big deal.*

c)   *When I hired my first employee.*

Did their vision of the business change at all over the course of the first year?

a)   *Completely, one idea morphed into another new business.*

b)   *Too much or lack of sales made me change my focus.*

c)   *No, I followed my Action Plan in my Business Plan.*

What would they do differently if they could do it over?

a)   *Have more capital for the start-up.*

b)   *Work on the business not in it.*

c)   *Not give up my day job!*

I've given this questionnaire to over 900 entrepreneurs. I was always amazed to see that of the 2700 business people interviewed by my clients the answers almost always revolve around the ones above. I think the answers are insightful!

Passion & Timing

I like to think there are two prerequisites that are no brainers when it comes to deciding whether or not you take the leap from that cozy, no-end in sight, badly managed, dead-end job to your new business endeavour. Sure you'll soon be wondering where your next contract will come from or when your next customer will walk through the door of your shop; but you will be self employed.

The two considerations are **Passion** and **Timing**!

Ahh, a mouthful and a lot of considerations you think and you are right. OK, I'll get to Passion and Timing in a minute. Realistically do you have the knowledge to start your own business, the finances, a USP (unique selling point), the necessary skill sets? These are the basics but you still need passion and timing.

When I was a kid of 10 I fell in love with cameras and photography. As I matured into adulthood I kept my passion for photography alive as a hobby and even made some money at it. When I turned 30, circumstances (timing) allowed me to take the big plunge, the risk, the black hole, the abyss – self employment. On a wing and a prayer I started my photography business after falling out with a bad boss and a very stressful job as a Federal Parole Officer.

Boy, my first studio was $150 a month and close to home. All I had in this 3000 sq. ft. warehouse space was a simple 9 foot backdrop, a desk, a tripod and a light – I had it made in the shade. I had acquired my Independence!

It was a disaster and a total waste of money but insights from friends, self-realization and diminishing money had me realize after a year that I needed a game plan. With a plan in place, I eventually created a successful photography business which evolved into an ad agency including web development and multimedia print production with an international reputation.

The thing that kept me going was the **Passion** I felt for what I did. I loved photography and was sure I couldn't do it anymore if I lost the passion. I eventually came to that place many years later when I realized I didn't want to go into the digital age and closed my high end studio in the center of Vancouver. My passion had certainly diminished and when the fun was gone it was time for me to close my business and find a new venture.

Timing is the second major personal consideration. Call it luck, call it karma but timing comes easily for some and for most of us it evades us like water in a desert. A young man came to my office a couple of months ago and proudly said he wanted to import 'Razor scooters' that had 2 neat little wheels and folded up to fit into your trunk or backpack. He told me his girlfriend had a great deal lined up in China – only $49.95 each.

I reminded him that they were in fashion 15 years ago and his timing was off. It had come, and unfortunately, gone for him and his product. Besides when it first came to Canada it was $200 in the store but quickly went to $29.95 when the Chinese copied and mass produced them. The market as a phenomenon died!

I tell my new entrepreneur clients it's about their personal timing too.

If your friends and family tell you that you are crazy for wanting to be 'your own boss' maybe they know something about you that you're neglecting to consider. You really must want to be self employed and your family and friends <u>MUST</u> support your decision. In those dark days ahead you're going to need friends who are supportive and family who can handle an extra bill here and there while your business is struggling and growing.

Timing is also measured by the economy. Your product or service must be in demand so timing is a credible determinant as to whether you should be in business.

Selling beer in a recession/depression may be a great idea with good timing because people drink at home during those times, therefore its recession-proof. In 2009, when the economy was going to hell in a hand basket, I was negotiating to buy a national beer distribution company. The deal fell through but I thought it was a good idea at the time, because if my friends are any indication, when people are depressed they drink.

Selling luxury autos during a recession is a good idea but selling mid prices vehicles like Mustangs or Acura's fall flat because people with money still have money but people on the edge buy cheap.

You may notice that restaurants like MacDonald's thrive in a recession as well as super high-end restaurants. People lacking money eat frugally at fast food restaurants more often and rich people who can hold onto their cash can afford to still visit the high-end establishments. I can guarantee that mid-priced restaurants have suffered in a bad economy.

And you thought it was just about opening a shop and customers will come... ha!!

Things to Consider Before You Quit Your Job

Do You Hate Your Job? I must tell you I've never really hated a job I worked at but I despised a boss or two, not that I have had that many. To be stuck in a job that is taking a person nowhere, which is full of endless aggravation from a micro-manager or having a boss who is an idiot must drive people to drink. I can't imagine working under a boss like that for years until retirement but many do.

How are You with Time Management? I have a client who determined at the outset of beginning her home-based business that she would not accept calls from friends or family during her business day. She would not watch television or do housework to avoid ruining her business. She had a set work day, a home office complete with dedicated phone line and a lockable door. She had the perfect setup to avoid interruptions. Most of us have problems defining our time for work. I've had retired friends call me for a lunch at the pub, or a client suggest a golf day because he wants to get out of the office. It's tough to be dedicated to time management

Do You Need Capital & Where Will You Get It? We often forget about a startup budget, inventory to match demand, white boards, and office supplies when deciding to begin our businesses. Open the doors and they will come – marketing costs money. What resources do you actually have available in credit lines versus loans, can you borrow from family and friends? Know your limits and your available resources.

Be Prepared. Create a business plan. With that in place you have planned for unforeseen circumstances, changes in trends and price increases from your suppliers. It's not really a Plan B but it is some thought put into a contingency plan so you're not caught with your pants down.

You Must Be the Jack of All Trades in the Beginning. I've talked about Michael Gerber's EMyth enough for people to know that we all start off as a technician in our business. You won't have the money to pay others to work for you so you must have an understanding of accounting, your business, marketing and sales. Basic knowledge will get you through to the next step but knowing when to bring in pros or employees is imperative.

A SWOT Analysis. This is a very important step in any business plan and a personal favourite of mine to perform for new entrepreneurs. **S**- Your Strengths, **W**- Your Weaknesses, **O**- Opportunities in the market place and **T**- Threats that will bring your business crashing down or kill it before you have even begun. It's important to know how to mitigate the ones which you marked with an X.

Know Your Customers & Your Competitors. Unless you know who your customers are you shouldn't be in business – it's called demographics. A guy I shared an office with years ago showed me his business plan. He was selling computerized services to artists. He stated in his business plan that "there are 6 billion people in the world and 4 billion had computers" so they were his customers, lol. So he was truly an idiot. Almost as important is to know who your competition is and analyzing what they are doing to acquire customers and how this could be improved. Sun Tzu, the Chinese General and Strategist said "Know your friends and keep your enemies closer".

Are Your Friends & Family on Board? If your beer drinking buddies and your family aren't with you on this it will be an uphill battle. Friends love to distract you from your new business, some of it may even be jealousy – they don't want the status quo changed. If you have to go home to a nagging partner that will be detrimental to your business too. Ahghg, keeping everyone happy.

How Much Time are You Going to Give it? Let's be realistic, if you have a finite amount of money you have to know how long you can survive before you make money from your business. Unless you have a wonderful working wife who will pay the bills, be prepared to decide how long your resources can support the business or have an alternative resource for funding. The rule of thumb is to have capital to start and at least 6 months to operate your business.

Is it Really Just a Hobby? Make sure that your business isn't really just a hobby. I have seen too many people who are in love with their products or services and essentially sign up for a lifetime of poverty by opening their business as their only source of income. I have had several of these guys/gals as clients at any point in time. They are just too stubborn to take a part time job to supplement the income from their business, which is really part-time and always will be. Sometimes it's just really important to be honest with yourself, understand that it is a hobby which gives you extra cash.

Keeping Your Options Open. It's so nice to be able go back to your old job if the business fails after a few months, so don't leave in a bad state of mind or beat that terrible boss over the head with his laptop. Sometimes it is an option to go back to your old job because let's face it; some people just can't make it as an entrepreneur.

Just remember starting a business is a milestone in your life. Use any tools at your disposal to determine if all your ducks are in a row before leaving that comfy day job.

Chapter Three
One Idea, One Business

Startup or Buy an Existing Business?

I've got you all hyped up so far with starting your own business from an idea -right? Well let's throw in a wrench – do you really want to start your NEW business from scratch or should you buy someone else's established business.

Wow, what a conundrum! Do I put tons of time in to developing a business from scratch and face overwhelming odds at failure or do I buy someone else's jewel of a business with tons of money? Hmm.

It's so nice to setup your own business based on your own dream with your own systems and with all your own peccadilloes. On the other hand you could buy a ready-made business already making money and have a better than average chance at success.

Or do you?

All things being equal, we can assume the latter choice, that of buying a business, is a well run business, generating good revenues and is a sure bet. Now take away the 'all things being equal' notion. You could be buying the proverbial pig in a poke, in other words a bad business that will drown you in a sea of someone else's problems that are now yours.

My bet is your dream, albeit, tougher to produce, is a better choice in most situations. Remember that the business you are contemplating buying was someone else's dream business. Systems (if any) were developed by the previous owner and all of his bad habits are also ingrained in <u>his</u> dream business.

What, oh what, to do?

It's called due diligence and means research the heck out of every aspect of the proposed sale before putting your hard earned (or borrowed) money on the line. Every management consultant has stories of the client who came to them after they had purchased the business only to find extra partners, skeletons in too many closets to count and accounting managed by a mob boss.

A client bought a business after the owner told him sales were 35% more than actual figures and since the books had been 'cooked' the facts came out only after my client started running the under performing business. This can also go the other way. I had a client who wanted to sell his business but had run his business like he did in China using 'Chinese Accounting' (his words), meaning 2 drawers in the till, one dollar for the business and $2 for his retirement fund. What was the problem in this case? He earned $34,000 a month as a corner grocery store owner but claimed he earned $12,000. Imagine the look on his face when he tried to tell the prospective owner he had lied through his teeth to the tax authorities with no way to prove the higher numbers.

The things to learn from due diligence:

Why is the current owner selling such a masterpiece business?

What are the books telling you about the current financial status of the business?

If the business is not performing up to standards what factors are causing the problems?

What is the long-term potential given your new management?

Will your management style easily merge with the corporate structure?

What issues come with the current staff?

What is a fair and equitable price?

What are you prepared to offer? This is not an auction you will have time to make a considered offer? Be prepared to negotiate or have someone help you.

I sent one of my clients to the business he wanted to buy and made him sit in his car for 2 days with a clipboard and a counter. His job was to observe people walking by the store and counting people going in the door, counting at different times of day and observing the demographics of the people walking by.

BTW this is good advice when you are choosing a location for your own business.

I've walked into the businesses on either side of the business for sale to ask them for some 'inside' information and yes, even gossip. You'd be surprised when the guy next door tells you that the wife of the seller is leaving and he'll sell cheap because the divorce will clean him out.

How about going into the business as a customer to see how you're treated, how employees work, how others see the business?

Opportunist? You bet!

If you do your 'due diligence' it may make the difference between a good business opportunity and a dismal bankruptcy down the road. At least you will have a fighting chance.

If you feel buying an existing business is better for you, these 8 Points in Evaluating Buying an Existing Business will help.

Why is it Being Sold? - A friend of mine is retiring so it's a legitimate exit strategy but he is 67 and others I know are in their 30's and 40's. Why are they selling? Is it because the money is not there, is it poorly managed, a bad mix of product and owner, a bad product or worse?

Legal Considerations – Are there existing contracts or encumbrances owing on the business? Is there a lot of debt outstanding? A friend was all ready to buy a great business on paper until I told him about a silent shareholder who had a criminal history who certainly brought bad karma to the deal. The $5 million deal stalled soon after my conversation.

Is it Financially Sound? – Have you seen the books, the real ones? Has the owner taken a salary or had the company pay all his expenses? Are there strange entries in the books he's given you to read? I had a friend who paid his 2 year old son to valet park cars for his butcher shop, looked great on his tax return. I've also seen clients with 2 sets of 'books' which were hundreds and thousands of dollars apart in numbers.

Market Value – Many consider the value of a business at 2-3 times net profit. I have a client who sees a very, very liberal $50k in net but is trying to sell his business for $600K. He is listing it at what he thinks it is valued without considering a realistic price. It's only worth $200k.

Is it Right for You? - I have another client considering buying a bakery/cafe in a remote part of the country, not knowing the market, the area or the product. Would it not be prudent to buy a business you enjoy, have knowledge of, have a passion for or use the product?

Assets – Are the assets listed in the books old and need replacing? Are the assets enough to manage growth or will you need to upgrade or add to existing assets to increase sales?

Leases – I have a client who wanted to purchase a very exciting coffee shop well established in a good location in New York City. The price was right but the lease upon scrutiny shows only a few months left on the lease. The coffee shop owner assured him the property owner would renew for 5 years plus a 5 year extension. What he didn't say was that Starbucks was eyeing the property and was willing to increase the rent by 20% to get the lease. Ouch!

Balance Sheet- This point goes hand in hand with number 3 above. You can see the chart of accounts of a business, see their journals and spreadsheets but have you seen the profit/loss sheets? Make sure you see all the documents before you sign, even more so if you have fallen in love with the property. This leads me to another point – don't fall in love with an opportunity!

Working on Your Business Not In It

I hate the phrase self-employment. It identifies you as a person who is running their own business, correct?

Well I hate the words. It sounds like you have created a 'job' for 'yourself' forever destined to be doing it by yourself.

I like the term 'Entrepreneur'. It sounds so dramatic, mysterious, sophisticated and perhaps unique. It makes us feel like perhaps we may be able to tread in the footsteps of 'the Donald' (Trump) or even have the capability to run an international conglomerate.

Michael Gerber, the famous Business Consultant and writer of the invaluable E-Myth series of books on business made note of two major theories; '*systems for the operation so you are working on your business not in it*' and '*being the entrepreneur in the business not the technician*' are legendary.

Gerber says you should setup systems for your business as if it is a MacDonald's in the making. Imagine setting up your systems so that anyone could run your company if you weren't around. A photographer client of mine has DVD's showing how to do his photography techniques. He also has procedures manuals setup with everything from how to greet customers at reception to making sales and how to store images and media.

He didn't think he was going to franchise when he set the systems in place in his business but after 30 years he now has 6 franchises.

In each new entrepreneur there are 3 different mindsets in the operation of the business- the Technician, the Manager and the Entrepreneur.

In every Entrepreneur there is the Technician, the guy who does the work, the Manager who runs the business and the Entrepreneur who does the thinking.

Every business owner starts at the Technician phase but many don't progress past it.

A business owner has to progress through those phases; doing the work until an employee can replace you, you then become the manager. Once you've got a couple of employees or more you may find that one is really good at his/her job. You make this person the manager so he can take over the operation of the business. When you replace yourself as manager you then become the thinker, the guy with the direction – the Entrepreneur. Now, with the business almost running itself it's time for you to go golfing.

Let's say you start a new automotive garage, guess who does the work on the cars? You do – because you own the company and you're the only employee you have; so far- you are the Technician.

So you get a little busy and after working yourself half to death you decide to hire a couple of employees. Now they are the technicians and you become the Manager.

So you manage your new business for months or years until your several technicians (employees) start to wear you out and you find an outstanding technician who is leadership material. You make him the Manager.

Since you have replaced yourself as the Technician and the Manager you now become the Entrepreneur.

Let's put this in perspective. The Technician is the employee in a normal corporation; the Manager could be compared to the President of the company and the CEO is the Entrepreneur. The President manages the daily operations of the business and the CEO/Entrepreneur is the thinker, the head of the organization.

My buddy owns a huge photography company. He is the CEO/Entrepreneur.

He's an unusual guy. He likes to watch late movies on his big screen TV in his large home in a suburb of Vancouver so he sleeps in till 11 am. Twice a week his schedule changes and his trainer will wake him at 10. Normally he gets up and has his coffee, shower, reads the paper and around lunch time he goes to his basement and opens the non-descript glass door to... his business operation!!

He opens the door and inside are 10 people working hard on computers where they are proofing photographs, printing pictures and outputting thousands of photo orders per day (sometimes there are 3 shifts of these workers per day). They have been there since 8 am.

He calls over to Dave, his dedicated Manager, and asks him how things are going. Dave replies as usual that everything is under control. The CEO is doing his job. Everyone has work to do and it is running smoothly. Rents will be paid, cars will be maintained, families will have food, homes will have paid mortgages and the best thing – customers will be happy. This is another day in the life of a successful business.

The CEO, happy his staff is working and the fact that his Manager is managing leaves the workplace after 15 minutes in the 'office'.

Golf called his name. He used to golf but as an Entrepreneur it holds little interest after a while – my friend, the CEO/Entrepreneur needs a challenge.

He called me a while ago and told me he had started a flower shop up the street from his 'office'. I asked him what he knew about running a flower shop. I've been his friend for decades and although he is a nice guy, he is a man's man, gruff, big, and aggressive (you know the type) - like an FCC fighter. It was a shock for me and it was obvious. He looked at me knowing my thoughts and said that he had already hired a manager and 2 florists because "what do I know about flowers".

He is an Entrepreneur! I can't wait to see his next business.

Michael Gerber is a man who understands what it means to be an entrepreneur and how to walk the walk having done so for around 40 years. I have been inspired by Michael for many years after he hired me to be his personal photographer when he was on a speaking engagement to Vancouver over the course of 3 days many years ago. He gave me a tape of the E-Myth and that set me on my current course of *Working On the Business Not In It.*

Having said that it is not an easy feat to suddenly stop working doing the job you may like and having others do it for you. Giving up control to gain control is a strange statement but very true. If you give up being the technician to manage the business you will have taken the biggest step towards being an entrepreneur with absolute control.

Imagine you are a plumber who has dedicated 25 years with your current employer. Friday before Labour Day you get a layoff notice - so much for Labour Day. But hey you are a certified, qualified, expert plumber, what do you have to worry about? After two weeks on the couch your wife asks you when you will be getting your ass off the couch and finding a job. Hey, it's only been two weeks! You look for a job for a month, getting more and more discouraged as you are told you're over qualified, or worse, no one tells you, that yes, you are too old. Aghgh. Now what?

You go out and get some business cards printed up then decide to hang out your own shingle announcing your new plumbing business. Only costs you a business card to setup your business, amazing. So after 25 years of climbing under houses, fixing toilets, installing bathtubs and cleaning drains you're back to doing it for yourself. 'How great!' you think, if I want I can go golfing anytime I want, if only you golfed, or go to that great lake you know of to fish. The reality is that business is not that plentiful and to make a good income you have to work day and night – and weekends, working on those same toilets and drains; so much for the big dream. You now know what working IN your business means.

OK, now let's look at it from a different perspective using me for an example. Take the same plumber scenario with 25 years in the trenches, no pun intended and that big layoff.

I'd take a couple of weeks to relax around the house like the first guy and after I'd gotten bored watching CNN every day I'd evaluate my options. The only similarities between me and the first plumber is that we were laid off and started a company. Of course, I'd start a plumbing business but instead of printing business cards with Gary C. Bizzo – Plumber, it would say Gary C. Bizzo – CEO.

I'd go down to the little pub where I know my former colleagues at ACE Plumbing hang out after work and make my list of a few guys who I'd like to work for me. Yes, you heard it, work for me. I'd pick some young talented guys I liked and respected then make them an offer to work for me at a little better salary; after all I have no overhead like the big company.

These young guys with renewed inspiration, which I would help instill in them, would go to work with a gung ho attitude for me. They are finally getting what they are worth and working for a great guy, lol.

I'm not working alongside them I'm managing them from the outset; after all, I'm tired of crawling under houses and fixing toilets. I'm in phase 2 of the triumvirate Technician, Manager and Entrepreneur. My goal is to get to the Entrepreneur stage where I oversee everything and focus on planning and strategies for growth.

I keep my eye on the three young guys I hired looking for enthusiasm and talent over and above the rest. After a few months I make my choice and promote the best guy to Manager to replace me. Phew, did I really give control of my company to a young guy not yet 30 years old? Sure did!

That means I am the Entrepreneur as there's nowhere to go from here. I can delegate to my heart's content but my main goal is to allow him to run the day to day operations of the business while I think of the big picture. Heck, I may even open a franchise or another business unrelated to plumbing as long as he is capable.

So would you rather work On or In your business?

When I was working with Gerber in 2011 on a new concept 'The Dreaming Room' in Vancouver, the concept of the entrepreneur progressing from the worker through to the CEO was on the top of our list to get out to the masses. Michael added a new kink to the concept since he wrote the EMyth in the 1970's – he's added a new aspect, paying it forward. An altruistic concept, Paying It Forward in his mind means that when you become successful don't forget to give something back to the community that helped you get there. It's a mantra I try to live by for sure.

Focus

Some people are able to multi-task quite well. I'm lucky to be one of those types. You really need to be able to focus when it comes to running a business. You must be doggedly determined to let nothing come between you and your business. Quite often a person will ask me for advice by saying, "I have these great business ideas". No, no, and no - please stick to the best one and only one.

You may have several ideas rattling around in your mind but realistically you need to identify which one has the most reasonable amount of success, which one you will enjoy the most, which idea is the easiest to implement and which one are you able to fund properly.

Another serious issue is which business idea are you fundamentally attached too with a large amount of passion associated to it?

If you learn and develop the skills to run a business you can operate any type of business down the road once your primary business is established.

I have several businesses but they are wrapped around a common theme - marketing. Any one of my companies can be, and some are, subsidiaries of the main business. I have a deep love for business so that is my main 'focus', however, I also love social media networking and I am really, really good at that so I tell my wife my 'vocation' is business and my avocation (hobby) is social media. That allows me work more hours in the day because one is my hobby, lol.

Naming Your Business

I like to tell my clients to be very careful choosing their business name and I actually do a workshop on the topic. A good friend of mine told me of his new company name, *Dubble Exxpress Go*. Now anyone would have the devil of a time finding this in the phone book because rightly so the spelling is not usual for those words no matter how disjointed or perhaps inebriated a person may be. My friend, Xerxes, is a lovely guy and the fact that he is from India should not be relevant to his choice of business names but wait – imagine for a moment Xerxes answering the phone in an excited East Indian accent.

He gets so excited talking to customers his English is sometimes difficult to hear and understand clearly. I quickly offered to remedy the situation by producing a website for him so that his customers would find him through the web versus the phone book. With some good SEO and my flair for picking names, lol, I created a website called www.vancouvervendingmachines.com.

Does this leave anything to the imagination as to what Xerxes actually sells? Yes, his product is vending machines but he doesn't sell them he places them in businesses free of charge and people only pay for the product which he diligently collects once a week with a smile and his high-spirited personality. I love this guy, but geez, the name leaves much to be desired. When you type in his website it comes up nicely with his Dubble Exxpress Go name and his unique logo. At least I had my input on the website.

Something meaningful?

I've noticed that my Asian clients like to name their businesses with something familiar and meaningful to them. How many "Golden" restaurants or "Win Win" or "Double Win Enterprises" are there out there? Golden Bell may sound good for a Chinese food restaurant, but doesn't have the same impact for a petrochemical consultant. My client wanted to be considered a North American educated consultant and in a very serious business like oil and gas, first impressions are important.

We came up with Stonebridge Consulting, giving an image of strength (a bridge of stone), longevity and Anglo Saxon for sure. Headquartered in Vancouver, her business sounds like it has been around for years.

Her sales went from $5000 a month to $40,000/month within 6 months. I attribute it mainly to the strong name and branding we did for her.

Use your own name?

Using your own name can bring other headaches. Startups love to have their name in the business name, but what if your name is Bilodeau (like the Canadian Olympian). People will get caught up in the spelling and give up. Now, if your name was Foster, it might be different. Anyone for a beer?

Think from your customers' perspective

The bottom line is; be careful, think from your customers' perspective, check if there is anything close from other business' and use commonsense. Remember your name will be with you a long time.

Some obvious and legal issues to Consider

Your business name should be carefully thought out and a lot of things you may not have considered should be taken into account. Here are a few things that I teach in my Marketing series that might give you some ideas for a better business name;

Does it incorporate a descriptive element, unique element and a defining element, e.g. Healthex Pharmaceuticals Inc.?

Is it unique to be identifiable to customers, clear and recognizable?

Does it exhibit the right image, professional or otherwise as intended?

Stonebridge consulting exhibits power and longevity

Does it exhibit size correctly, e.g. sounds bigger than it is or smaller than it should be?

Does the name have legs for expansion, e.g. Futura Clothing versus Futura Kids Wear?

Does it take into account cultural differences? Asians may call it 'Golden Restaurant' or 'Win Win' enterprises but those names sound silly in Canada.

Can you secure the website to match the name? You can't get IBM.com for Integra Bio Management.

Can you secure a name that represents the business name without identifying it, e.g. VancouverVendingMachines.com takes you to Dubble Exxpress Go Ltd.?

Does a name really matter? A company can be a number.

Do you really, really love the name; it's yours for a long time?

How does the name sound when the owner answers the telephone?

Is the spelling unusual, can it be found on the internet, e.g. Dubble Express Go Ltd.?

Does the name have significance to the business owner and does it reflect that to the customer?

Should you use your own name or is that too arrogant? Using your own name works if you're a designer, professional or trying to get cachet from your name or reputation.

Is there a copyright infringement in the name and colors used?

Look at it from your Customers point of view? Does the name sound interesting, reliable, and familiar?

How about Numerology, hey - anything to make it successful.

Research the name for any past issues?

...and here are some past issues using the wrong names:

There have been some monumental blunders in marketing history. **Hoover**, the well known maker of vacuum cleaners, sells a model on the European market, including Germany, called the **Zyklon**.

Zyklon is the German word for Cyclone, so it is a seemingly sensible choice for a powerful vacuum. However, Zyklon B was the lethal gas used by Nazis in concentration camps during WW2.

Meanwhile, CNN.com reported on August 28, 2002, that British shoe maker **Umbro** received many protests for its running shoe the Zyklon. Umbro apologized and renamed it. Apparently, the shoe had been named the Zyklon since 1999, but they had not written the name on the shoe until recently.

A week later, BBC News reported that **Bosch Siemens Hausgeraete (BSH)** was withdrawing its trademark application for the name Zyklon. BSH had filed two applications with the US Patent & Trademark Office for "Zyklon" across a range of home products, including **gas ovens**.

When you choose the name of your business remember that this is your baby, yours to have and to hold for as long as you are in business. So make it memorable or at least make it something you can relate to or feel good about.

I remember in the 1980's going to a Numerologist friend of mine for help choosing the name of my new photography business. After much discussion, back and forth, we compromised with Bizzo Photography & Design. Yes the ampersand (&) was critical to the correct numbers. I think my friend would have been happier if we had just changed my name to Caleb Smythe or something.

Seven Tagline (slogan) Ideas for Your Business

The tagline or slogan follows the name usually beneath the name and may be in italics, or not, or another manner to differentiate. This is then analyzed under the following criteria:

Does it correctly identify the nature of the business?

Does it include words not in the title of the company name?

Does it reflect quality, benefits or price differentiation?

Should you put dots between specific points?

Should you use italics or a different color to differentiate?

Should you try to be funny? That depends on the customer. A client ABC HiRise Caulking loved his company tagline *"The Fastest Caulk in the West"*. His clients were usually men who thought that was hilarious.

Pitfalls to avoid:

Taglines that are too long;
Words above a grade 6 education level;

Repeating words in the business name in the tagline ;
Obscure words or double meanings; and
Rude or silly words.

Basing Business on Solutions to a Problem

Don't try to be all things to all people. Finding a business niche and sticking to it allows you to find a problem and fix it, a need that no one is addressing and/or a product or service that exceeds the quality of an existing business. Unless people want your product or service, no-one will buy it until necessity drives them there.

There's a really great store in my neighbourhood which sells everything. I'm sure it started off as a flower shop, but it has progressed into a flower shop which also sells unique coffee tables and lamps, novelty items, expensive jewelry, greeting cards, wall hangings, lighters, phone cards and even cigarettes.

This diversity must have its roots in the past when business was slow and they needed to find and inventory anything that would sell. Some of their merchandise is cheap products from abroad but many are very expensive items ranging up to hundreds of dollars. Most businesses rely on the fact they can buy quantity at a cheap wholesale price and sell it at a higher price. If you have a store filled with small volume items your margins have to be lower.

This little store is a great place to browse while the flowers I purchase are wrapped but all the products are impulse items. I will buy something because it inspires me or hits the buyer urge in me when I see it. It's unlikely that I will go there for the sole purpose of buying an eclectic product.

Businesses are created, survive and reach sustainability because they answer the need of the consumer, the client, the customer. In *Field of Dreams*, the classic line was "if you build it they will come", ha. There are a lot of factors that go into a statement like that for a new business. Does the business fill a need? Is it different, cheaper or totally unique?

If you open an ice cream store in Alaska you may like ice cream a lot but you may not be filling a need considering summer is only a couple of months a year and most people consider anything warm as 'comfort food'.

Chapter Four

The Nuts & Bolts

What Makes a Great Business Plan?

I am a strong believer in writing a strong, concise, honest and factual business plan that can find you an investor, close a deal, give you direction and goals, or give you accountability. After all, it is a strategic plan. I tell my clients they can do several things with the plan after it is written. They can fire it into a garbage can, file it for future reference, modify it every month or think of it as a changing document that can grow with them and give them direction. All of these options are correct by the way, because the part of the business plan that is important is the writing of it. Once you have written your ideas on paper it's indelibly etched in your mind.

I've put a Business Plan template at the end of this book in the Appendix but here are some considerations to keep in mind.

A Clear and Realistic Financial plan

You must realize that a banker, an investor or possible partner is going to want to be able to understand the basic financial position of your business. You should be able to put together a Start-up budget and have the basic skills to put together a pro forma (forecast) for the next 2 years of your business. Please don't make things up.

Detailed Market Research

Do you know the type of customers you want to attract, the size of your market and what those people expect or want from you? Have you done your market research? Have you developed your demographic analysis and your psycho-graphics?

Competition Analysis

Have you identified not only your customers but also your competitors? You have to know what your competition gives their customers in order to compete effectively.

A Good Management Team

The CEO of an international corporation, and friend, once told me an entrepreneur needs three things to have a successful business; money, good management and a good product. If you have any two of the three you can find the third, e.g. if you have a great product for sale and money you can find the management team.

Serious Forethought Throughout

You really need to have put some thought into the whole plan. Have you considered your pricing, your distribution channels, suppliers, cash flow and your handling of its' growth or lack thereof?

Scalability

You should be able to handle slow growth and slower sales. You need to develop a plan that allows for a scalable business. If you need $50,000 in financing to run the company can you run it effectively if you can only get a loan of $25,000? Having scalability allows you to be able to maneuver through tough times and grow or contract when needed. Banks like to see scalability and will often give you a portion of what you need not the entire amount.

The Executive Summary

In your Executive Summary the questions you need to ask yourself and answer are: who, what, when, where, why and how much money you'll make or need to have. If you are going to the bank for financing, the analyst will most likely read your executive summary and decide upon that one page whether he will read further, so you need to give them a hook on that first page.

Professionalism

Let's assume if you are going to a bank for financing you need a minimum of $50k for your company to go further. You better have a professional looking plan in place. Cirlox bound, written in the 3rd person and in a 12 pt. type. You need to have an appendix of supporting documents including resumes, job descriptions and copies of websites, etc.

Writing Your Business Plan to Secure Money?

Keep the written plan size to a reasonable length, with a maximum of 25 pages not including appendices with all relevant documents, like resume, research, etc.

The Business plan represents your company and you, so make it look great, bind it, use graphics and make sure there are no typos.

Keep it conservative but optimistic especially with your financials.

Make an appointment at the bank or credit union before you go.

Forward the banker you are meeting a copy of the business plan for them to review before they meet you. They'll check your character, collateral/credit and cash flow so be prepared.

They send your application off to an analyst to do a Risk assessment. The Risk assessment will include research on how the economy is, timing, competition, industry going to affect the business failing or not.

Do you have cash flow coming in a reasonable time on your financial forecast? The lendors want to know you can pay the loan. The proforma will tell them at a glance.

Are you going to purchase assets that the bank can use to protect their money? They like that.

Involve your accountant and other professionals in your plan to reassure uneasy bankers. They like to know you have these people in place and can use them as a resource when needed. It's also good to have a credible Advisory Board.

Take the banker meeting as a way to form a relationship because if you fail to get money from him, he may have access to alternative financing channels into which you can tap. At the very least, he can tell you why you didn't get the loan so you can improve your next application.

If you get the money - spend it wisely!

Business Plans - an Immigrant's Perspective

I was thinking about the problems newcomers to Canada face when trying to setup a business. In past magazine articles I've talked about cultural differences, support groups and finding a business you can relate to probably from past experience or skills you've learned in your home country.

I think it is important to discuss the planning of your business, the strategies defining your market and the method in which you will approach the necessary steps in setting up your new business as an entrepreneur.

The Business Plan Essentials

The Business Plan is your guide, your friend and sometimes your nemesis but always it will guide you, remind you of problems you will face and it will define you as an entrepreneur. It will make or break your business.

The Business Plan format and template is easy to find, go to any bank (RBC has a nice one) and you will find a template with easy to answer questions allowing you to fill in the blanks – but wait a moment, it really is not that easy.

Of course, the easy part is the **Vision** of your business. The **Mission** statement is also not complicated. The Vision is how you see your business in 5 years. In defining your Vision, think of all your dreams, goals and how you always thought a business should look like if you had the opportunity to own and run one. Assuming you open a shop, you might decide that your business will have more than one location, have a certain number of employees and have revenues high enough to provide you with an adequate lifestyle. Write it down, it might only take a paragraph but it needs to be meaningful and attainable to you.

The Mission is how you see the company being run and its purpose. Your purpose in relation to a shop could say "all our products are guaranteed, our employees are of the highest caliber and we are recognized in our city as being the best place to go for the best service and product". Your mission should be clear, socially meaningful and measurable so you know when you have reached your goals.

The **Personnel Plan** defines who is running the company and the type of employees you will hire. It also describes your forecasts for future growth in terms of employees. Often when you are writing a business plan the last thing people think about is "How do I deal with success?" Most focus on getting the sales yet few prepare for it. You need to be prepared for the growth of your business, how you see employees being utilized and alliances in the business community who may help you.

A t-shirt manufacturer client had no plan for growth so when he received a huge order for a festival he was caught without enough staff to produce the quantity that was needed. He had to subcontract the job to another company and lost a great deal of money because he was unprepared.

The personnel plan will be an asset when you are going to a bank seeking a loan as it defines who the people are who manage the company as well as the support in the business community you may have to keep your success and your business on track.

You can add your strategic alliances and your advisory board here as well. Get quality advisors, they will impress the bankers.

Financial Statements are still financial statements whether you are in India, China or Vancouver. You know your product and what it costs to sell so the only thing holding you back is how to put the sales/revenues on paper so you can track it and how to sell your product in Canada.

The Financial plan includes a start up budget which defines how much money you will need to open the doors to your business. This typically is facilities, equipment, materials and supplies that you will need in the beginning. Typically you can claim expenses in items for the company you purchased or leased within 6 months of your startup of operations.

Once you know how much you need to setup your company then all you need to do is calculate the money required to operate your business and to make a profit for you.

You then need to develop a cash flow forecast. Using a spreadsheet you need to create an income/expense statement that shows by month where your revenues and expenses will come and the expenses associated with it. Using an Excel spreadsheet you can quickly make minor changes to costs and revenues to see how the 'bottom line' is affected. While the Marketing plan is important most feel keeping an eye on your expenses and revenues by your spreadsheet is the most important aspect of your business plan.

Enter your **Marketing Plan**; the Marketing plan is often the stumbling block for newcomers. You're in a new country with new standards, new ways of doing things and certainly a new attitude about doing business than what you are used to in your home country. Your home may have been big on brochures and newspapers to send your message to prospective clients. You may find that your product is best marketed in Canada, by word of mouth or social media networking. You will need to consult professionals to see which method works in your specific industry. It is worth the extra money to talk to professionals about marketing techniques than to go fast and furious on a marketing program that will not meet Canadian standards or fall within the usual ways of reaching customers.

One of the first things to do is create a **SWOT** Analysis. Don't worry this is easy! On a page write Strengths, Weaknesses, Opportunities and Threats and then under each write what you feel is important to you and your business. Strengths and Weaknesses are internal and relate to you. It's good to know your personal strengths but more importantly to know your weaknesses as once you have identified them you can figure out a way to reduce their effect on your new business. A good example of a weakness is lack of sales ability. To reduce this as a weakness you can consider hiring a salesperson and include that cost in your start up budget.

Opportunities and Threats relate to external forces you have no control over but need to know. If you have decided to start a business you must have identified a need in the community and the opportunity to make a living. You must equally consider the Threat in the community as this may cause trouble to arise. A client asked for advice when negotiating a lease for a coffee shop on a popular street corner in downtown Vancouver. The location with large pedestrian traffic seemed like a great opportunity. The threat was Starbucks who wanted the same location. Starbucks of course, was a better choice as a tenant for the leasing agent. You need to know and understand all the threats.

Your demographics need to be addressed when finding a location for your business. Demographics are the type of data used to determine who will buy your product. Commonly it's age, race, gender, employment status etc. You need to setup your shop in a place whose demographics suit those who will purchase your product or service.

Psychographics contrast demographics. Psychographics are attitudes, personality, interests, activities and opinions of the customer. You may have a client base of 55-65 year old people as demographic who have a psychographic of being baby boomers, who are health conscious and are resisting retirement. A good combination of a study of both will identify your customer and make it easier to sell to them.

A Chinese client wanted to open a restaurant in a part of Vancouver which is mainly Caucasians who are health conscious. Her restaurant is a specialty Chinese dish liked mainly by Mainland Chinese people. She chose her location because it was close to her home not because it was close to her specialty market. This was a recipe for failure.

An **Action Plan** is the no nonsense method to set your goals when setting up your business. Putting your goals in writing with a plan on when you plan to attain them is a major step in providing a follow through plan to opening and operating your company. Be specific and realistic in your action plan. A good example is creating an action plan by month with one goal of creating your business cards with a cost attached to it. The next item may be your website started with a completion date. Remember the Action plan is broken down by month and takes you and your business over the next 12-18 months or so as a concrete plan to attain these goals.

Going to the bank requires the best prepared plan you can put together. The bank wants to see the personnel, your sales and marketing plan as well as your forecast for your revenues. With a good business plan, a local Credit Union (Vancity) will offer you a character based loan of up to $35,000 through their Be My Own Boss Loan program. If you are under 39 years old, the Canadian Youth Business Foundation will provide inexpensive loans up to $45,000. Traditional lending options exist for you but typically are based on credit worthiness and whether you own your own home or have other assets.

It is often said that the best laid plans fail because of lack of planning, for newcomers, the marketing of a product is more important than the price or the uniqueness of that product to the Canadian public.

People define how your business makes money or not, whether your product lies on a shelf or not and you must tune in to their needs. Spend your time writing a solid business plan.

What Form of Business Will You Have?

A lot of people will start a business and immediately run out and incorporate their company. This may or may not be the best way to proceed. I think there are two thoughts on this. What are the risks the owner may face and is there potential for a great deal of money being realized from this business?

A <u>Sole Proprietorship</u> is an unincorporated business that has been name searched and registered as such. In my area, the name search and registration will cost you $40 each. The owner is liable for any issues arising from the operation of his business and being that it is the simplest form of business it does not offer a lot of protection. Tax implications are easy too. Revenues from the business go into the individual's tax return and business expenses come off the total revenue.

A <u>Corporation,</u> listed as Inc., Incorporated, Ltd., Limited or Corporation as the business designation is the most protective form of business ownership.

The corporation provides protection against liability issues and quite often is used in situations where the business may encounter litigious customers, e.g. food preparation, restaurants, import/export, etc. Most suppliers and banks will ask the owner of the corporation to sign a personal guarantee because one of the features of the corporation is that the corporation is considered its' own entity able to own property etc., and as such, if anything happens to the company the owner does not have liability. The incorporation process takes about 30 minutes and costs about $300 dollars if you do it yourself. Most people like to use a lawyer to be on the safe side.

When it comes to liability, I recommend that if you are going into a business which can affect the health or personal issues of your customers than you should incorporate, e.g. a restaurant or travel agency.

<u>Partnerships</u> can be great if the partners have complementary skills (e.g. a photographer and a salesman) and a horror show if they have the same skills, (e.g. 2 photographers competing for the cool shooting jobs with no one wanting to do bookkeeping).

I tell people to write job descriptions for each other so each know the expectations upon them so if there is conflict it can be resolved easier.

<u>Shareholders</u> can be partners holding up to 100% of a predetermined number of shares but this can be an opportunity to do it right the first time. If I had a partner I would have each partner take 40% of share and leave some left over to allocate to possible investors if needed.

Your Unique Selling Proposition or Point (USP)

USP is a marketing concept that was first proposed as a theory to explain a pattern among successful advertising campaigns of the early 1940s. It states that such campaigns made unique propositions to the customer and that this convinced them to switch brands. The term was invented by Rosser Reeves of Ted Bates & Company. Today the term is used in other fields or just casually to refer to any aspect of an object that differentiates it from similar objects.

You could consider the USP as the benefit to a customer doing business with you. This is different from your niche. The USP is the reason why a customer would buy from you versus the competitor down the street. I have a client who fixes any problem you may have with your office computer or software. He only works for businesses and will go to your office, that's USP #1.

Secondly he explains in simple terms what he is doing or has done to the client's computer and gives tips to the client to avoid a recurrence. People love his casual, non-nerdy approach to service and his manner allows him to create a genuine relationship with his client. None of the work he does is shrouded in mystery and clients call him back regularly. By the way, this entrepreneur charges 30-50% higher than the competition.

As an aside, my computer entrepreneur started the computer service company as an interim business while he waited for certification by the government for a product he developed. Entrepreneurs don't wait for anything or anybody.

Location, Location, Location, What Entrepreneurs Need to Know

Location Intelligence is one of the most powerful tools to help the entrepreneur in setting up a retail operation. You've no doubt heard of demographics and maybe even psychographics but there is an art to finding a location and the combination of all 3 is 'location intelligence'.

Demographics refer to the selected population characteristics as used in marketing or opinion research. Commonly-used demographics include race, age, income, disabilities, mobility, educational, home ownership, employment status, and even location.

In contrast, **psychographic variables** are any attributes relating to personality, values, attitudes, interests, or lifestyles.

Location Intelligence is the capacity to organize and understand geographic relationships and how they relate to business placement. By combining geographic- and location-related data with other business data, i.e. demographics and psychographics entrepreneurs can gain critical insights on where to locate their business.

A client came to me a couple years ago asking help to close a leasing arrangement for a hair salon in Vancouver. When I went to the shop it was 3 blocks from a major intersection in East Vancouver, a popular ethnic destination. Being a Hispanic woman, my client had identified the area as a good source of customers since the local population had a strong Spanish demographic. She further identified the area as a good psychographic profile because the surrounding stores made it comforting to shop and the stores also had focused on the ethnicity of the people in the area.

Houston we have a problem! The rent was 3 times cheaper than an available space at that good intersection three blocks away. It needed work which the leasing agent said forget about it, take it as is. Upon inspection what did we find? There were no other businesses in that block that could draw customers, walk in traffic was non-existent because people did not like to walk that far from the main shops and there was traffic/parking restrictions outside the shop. The shop was on the wrong side of the street. It was situated on the side of the street where cars coming into town at rush hour would find convenient. Many people go to a hair salon on the way home from work so it was on the 'wrong' side of the street. Besides, the sun shone on the other side of the street. Her side was always in shadow therefore colder.

We visited the vacant shop at 'the corner'. It was very expensive in the mind of my client. The realtor was very knowledgeable and the following Q & A showed her expertise was very valuable and based on research. With my blessing my client signed the lease to the more expensive location that, unlike the cheaper place, came with a new paint job, a month's free rent, new carpeting, and a really pleasant landlord with whom she could actually speak Spanish. She was happy yet scared to death about the risk

What risk? By choosing the right location with the critical intelligence gathering process she went on to develop a very successful hair salon that she only wished she had more space to expand.

The Elevator Pitch

The elevator pitch is an introduction about you and your business to another person in the 15-30 seconds it takes to go several floors in an elevator. It's also a metaphor for keeping the message short and sweet be it in an elevator, a networking event or a chance meeting with a prospective client.

Imagine the door to your Las Vegas hotel elevator opening on the 40th floor and in walks Donald Trump. He presses the Lobby and you have 40 floors to introduce yourself, pitch an idea or ask for money. Do you ask for an autograph, act like a Canadian and ignore him or introduce yourself?

How many times can someone try to improve on the elevator pitch? I won't try. I'll just explain the rationale behind it and give you a few tips to make life easier when meeting new people.

I've noticed in my dealings with my clients that many have great social skills at meeting people in a social situation but add their business into the equation and they are lost. It's funny but people seem to have a hard time explaining their business. It almost seems complicated when it should be second nature.

An elevator pitch includes who you are, what you are selling, why it is different and then you deliver the 'Call to Action' or what you want from your listener. The uses are numerous. You can use it at a networking event, in an email as an introduction or as a way of reducing your ideas to an essence like an executive summary.

When I first interview prospective clients typically they start to ramble about their business and the next thing I know they are telling me technical things and in no time it's tomorrow.

Forget about it! I tell them to distill their idea to 3 words. Hard to do. I had an interview that had my eyes glazing over while the guy was telling me about management styles, and controls, etc for 20 minutes without telling me the nature of his business. In a brilliant flash, like a eureka moment from an episode of *House,* I got it. "You're an Efficiency Expert!"

That's exactly what he was and I immediately showed him the door.

Seriously, you need to distill your idea into a succinct compact information tidbit. Here's my elevator pitch for my consulting company.

Hi I'm Gary Bizzo, I'm a Management Consultant working with X Public Company on the 40th floor. I'm finding lots of businesses are outsourcing to services like mine these days. If you ever have need of my services I'd like to give you my card

The trick is to keep your ideas simple so they come across easily and you make a simple yet effective introduction

Chapter Five

Finance - Show Me the MONEY

Financial & Business Goals

Control Your Cash.

Make a budget and stick to it. A lot of small businesses will open the doors knowing how much cash they have in the bank. Few know what the full cost of doing business is and most don't even know their break even point.

Set up a conservative budget based on a two year forecast, allow for realistic growth, a workable advertising allowance and follow your forecasts.

Big Picture While Keeping the Details in Focus

I've discussed the importance of having a focus, now I need to explain the big picture to you.

Harris Kern, a business writer, had this analogy to explain the big picture:

A traveler comes across three bricklayers on a scaffold. The traveler asks the first one, "What are you doing?" The first responds, "I am earning a wage."The traveler then asks the second one, "What are you doing?" The second responds, "I am building a wall". They are doing the same "work." Which of the two is laying the better brick? The traveler then asks the third one, "What are you doing?" The third responds, "I am building a cathedral".

The story illustrates the power that "big picture" thinking has on the everyday work of laying bricks. The bottom line is that everyone needs to see the Big Picture. This kind of thinking creates context and enables people to honor the values we seek to live and work by. People, typically, are not motivated by values alone. Instead, people are drawn to *outcomes*.

Planning for the startup period of 6 months and a 2 year budget forecast

I'm always telling you this important task and that, as it turns out all of these steps are important. An entrepreneur must tackle creating a budget for the new company, so you can see expected income, expenses and cash needs. Since you have history to rely on, you must create the budget using your best guess on income and expenses. This "how to" will focus on business with an inventory of products but it will also discuss a service business with no products.

Before you begin, consider why you need to spend the time to create a budget.

Even if you don't need bank financing, creating a budget is still a valuable exercise for any new and continuing business. Some of the things you will need to address are:

What do you need for the first opening day to make sales?

What facilities, equipment and supplies?

What are your monthly fixed expenses?

What are your variable expenses, e.g. commissions?

Can you create an estimate of sales?

Your two year budget is looking in the future at the business over the next two years and is typically called a proforma. A lot of people have trouble with this but if you take each piece of the budget one line item at a time it might look better than thinking the whole thing is too overwhelming.

I sometimes put the usual expenses in the budget like rent, hydro , telephone, etc. and then go to the end of the year and put a figure I'd like to earn that year and work backwards each month, e.g. $60k = $5000 a month. Hey, you can always hire a bookkeeper to help you setup your books. While he or she is setting them up you can have input into identifying your 'Chart of Accounts' which is the category list of expenses. If you really want to be in touch with your business this will be the defining factor by knowing the state of your finances.

Personal Goals

What do you want from being self employed? Do you want a job for yourself or to be an entrepreneur? You need to decide if the business is going to be long term, is going to make, to create the lifestyle you want. Will this business satisfy your personal needs, like ego and status? Make sure the personal goals in your business are achievable, worthwhile, and specific as well as connected to the growth of your business. Prioritize your goals and make them real to you. Just like New Year's resolutions you need to be vigilant and try hard to keep your goals. You need to constantly re-evaluate your goals and set rewards when you reach them.

Business Goals

Business goals are more like objectives and like personal goals need to be achievable, measurable and attainable. The fact that they are company goals makes it very meaningful to others involved in your business.

Specific goals that you attain in your business obviously can spill over to your private life. This may mean working fewer hours by hiring employees so you can spend more time with your family. A goal may be to increase your confidence skills so you can make more money and be happier making sales. A good example of a specific goal might be; "one month from now, I will spend entire weekends with my family by reorganizing my work schedule and learning how to delegate."

It has to be more than about the money.

Financing your Business

This has a wide variety of options with an equally wide array of issues associated with it. The rule of thumb is use OPM, Other People's Money, to finance your business. This may or not be your preferred situation.

Some people are quick to take their life savings and invest in their business. One of my clients sold her house to invest in her manufacturing business, went through all the money and is now left without a house. She could have secured third party financing and maybe if it was someone else's money she might have been more prudent.

The first stage of financing is finding money from family and friends. This is called the first round of financing and has been known to raise a considerable amount of money. If your family and friends won't invest in your business it might be an omen of what's to come.

If you want an Investor? What Will it Cost You?

If I had a nickel for every person that has **come** to me asking for investor help I would be able to invest in their business myself. Seriously though, most people don't have a clue what to ask for, what their business is worth or what to offer an investor once they have a live one in their hands.

A recent client asked me for help to secure an investor for an interactive children's website. With the excitement generated by Angry Birds, it's a hot market. I asked how much he wanted and he said a million. A million bucks? He had no cost analysis to back up the price and only said that it sounded like a great price for an incredible website experience. Hmm, wrong attitude guys. You need a detailed costing of exactly how much you will need to produce your product. You also need an analysis of what revenue model will work as well as the projected revenue streams and a plan to make your investor not only the money partner but an active one as well.

You need a feasibility study and/or a business plan. A well produced conservative business plan will give you the credibility in the eyes of the investor for him to make an educated consideration as to whether he wants to put money in your hands. People also fail to consider that most investors I know will invest on the gut feeling they get from the presenter. If you come across as a humble, logical person who has done your homework you will pass the first hurdle with an investor. Of course without the paperwork even the most genuine entrepreneur is unlikely to get a nibble from an investor.

Scalability is the way to have an ace up your sleeve. A client went to the bank looking for $150k to do a minor expansion in his warehouse, one that would make a considerable change to his margins by adding two lines of production people. The problem? The bank wasn't buying his evaluations and felt he might not be able to manage the payments. They offered him $100,000. Does he turn it down because it wasn't what he wanted? Not on your life. I had helped him develop a plan anticipating their reaction whereby we would scale the project down to keep pretty much the same space while still adding a second shift of workers not an entire production line. He got the money as a loan.

Bankers and investors are a diverse lot for sure. This brings the inevitable question of do you go to your local bank and get a loan, do you get an investor to buy into your business as a loan at a higher interest rate or do you give him equity in your company. Knowing your exit strategy puts control in your court.

I like to have an active investor; one who will give you money for a share of the company because now he has a reason to help you make it work and if he is willing he can give you his expertise as part of the deal. Sure as heck, more money will be needed and available if your investor has a 'hands on' attitude to your business success. To further clinch the deal I like the investor to have a firm hold on the finance of the business and usually suggest he brings his own Chief Financial Officer (CFO) as part of the deal.

Don't be afraid to give up control to the right investor. He's not about to mess up the business with his money in it and you are more likely to make money with his involvement. My attitude is 50% of nothing is nothing. I've seen so many guys fear the 51% rule only to lose a great partner. The funny thing is if you are running the business really well and are indispensable you are still in control of the business.

If you want to get investment money you need to plan, anticipate and be ready to negotiate. Amid all the doom and gloom out there I totally believe there are lots of guys with big money looking for a good deal. Conventional financing is next but most banks require you to provide collateral. They don't really want to see a business plan or pro forma promises. You may get lucky and find a jurisdiction in your community where banks will loan your business money based on your character. Character lending usually comes from a bank but is guaranteed through government programs. Little or no equity from you is required, you are not required to have collateral but you do need a business plan with a two year pro forma.

The previous two bank financing options need a good credit rating and FICO score. The last remaining source of financing is from angel investors. Angels are typically people who have access to liquid funds and are prepared to loan it to you for a higher than average percentage of return or for ownership in your business, usually about 30-40%.

Chapter Six

Marketing – The Art of Customer Acquisition

Marketing, Service, Quality

The success of your business will be a combination of these three items, marketing, service and quality. Your marketing puts your product and/or service out to the world. Service could be your unique selling proposition because most businesses seem to lack it. Quality is another differentiator and will help you decide on what pricing model is best for you and your product. If you are selling products that are inexpensive to buy your product may be more appropriate in a dollar store versus a high traffic/high cost per foot retail location.

Revenue Streams

Revenue streams refer specifically to the individual methods by which money comes into a company. A good balance of revenue streams can make a company and the lack of it will break your company in the same manner.

A corner store cannot be successful just selling milk and bread, that's why they carry a large array of products so they can have multiple sales streams. When they bring in the lotto terminals it's another revenue stream.

When I was a commercial photographer I had a revenue stream system. During the normal months when executives were in the office (fall, parts of winter and parts of spring) I would be able to conduct my commercial photography campaigns because there were senior executives around to make decisions. I liked commercial work because I usually only worked with the President and CEO of businesses.

I learned in the beginning of my career that if I only relied on Commercial work, even though it was very lucrative, I would have large gaps in my revenue and cash flow. I realized I could provide photography portraits for Christmas and Valentine's Day, and in

January I could book weddings for the summer months. My summer months therefore were booked solid with weddings at a time when my big executives took holidays and commercial work slowed to a crawl.

As I became well known in the industry as a competent commercial photographer I managed better paying accounts. One day I finished a big catalog shoot and asked the CEO what he intended to do with the pictures I had just done. He told me he needed to find a designer to produce his catalog. I told him not to worry I could give him a great quote on the full graphic and print production.

I had no idea what was required to put a catalog together so I hired a designer, found a production team and located a printer who put a first rate quote together allowing me to get a successful quote together. Another revenue stream was born!

From print I developed another revenue stream – the Internet and web pages. This was followed by the obvious transformation of my photography business/design studio into a boutique ad agency.

I had developed not only a multiple revenue stream in the photography niche but developed a revenue stream in the media production market.

I had a salesman who I asked to call on a large multinational corporation with 17 subsidiaries. He kept putting off calling the Marketing Department until I finally sat him down and had a conversation about revenue streams. He felt there was little we could do for him as far as photography was concerned. He said, "Look all I can get is some executive portraits".

I explained the process of finding revenue streams. I gave him the short list of work we could do for that specialized transportation business:

Product photography- they transported 140' concrete beams to build bridges and specifically designed trucks to do so

Executive portraits (which he had correctly identified) were out of date and needed to be redone

Art photography for the offices, nice big framed 'expensive' prints

Photojournalism at press conferences

Christmas parties

Family portraits at the Christmas party

Photos for brochures and newsletter

Retirement packages and parties

Art photos as gifts to clients

Website

Brochure

A published book on the company history

Annual report

Newsletter

I was so excited after running these possibilities at my salesman I met with the marketing guys the next day myself and secured a 3 year contract to be on call for all the revenue streams I had identified. I made $60K in 1986 just being on call with a pager on my hip working a max of 10 hours a month.

I would have still been there had this huge corporation not gone bankrupt (guess they paid me and others too much, lol)

Guerrilla Marketing Increases Business

I was pondering the different ways you can manage the promotion of your product, service and website. I'm a guerrilla marketer so pardon me if most of the guerrilla marketing tips are free if you have some skill at all in CRM or have someone to help you install a template at least for your blog.

Start off with a marketing plan; a guide to your focus and direction needs to be in place. When you develop your marketing plan you will have identified a few things necessary to have a successful operation. The obvious, a dynamic business name, a business card, snappy logo and a market niche can all be drawn into a compelling identity with a focused brand.

So how does a guerrilla develop a marketing plan? Let's try networking first, you will have to have something to say to the people you meet so make it interesting and there's that word again, compelling. Call this introduction to your business the 'elevator pitch'. Meeting people one to one is the best way to develop business. If you can convince the person on the opposite side of your conversation they will refer you to people they may know who needs your service. You should never try to sell the other person in a networking scenario. Think of it as word-of-mouth (WOM) referrals by a new friend to a friend of theirs. This WOM by a trusted friend is considered about 86% effective versus you trying to sell them.

Community involvement has always been one of the standards for getting business. If people see you in the community working you will have a reputation of someone who cares about something more than making money. Is it a wonder many businessmen join the Rotary or Lions Club?

Making you an expert is an interesting concept. Funny, but if people see you writing articles in local newspapers (editors are always looking for good articles) they think of you as an expert in your field and yes, they will look at you seriously as a supplier for them.

I used to joke to clients that they should find 4 friends and setup an association (you need 5) relevant to their business. For instance you are a Personal Organizer. Why not setup the Professional Organizers of British Columbia with you as the President or Executive Director of the association. Have a couple of friends as officers of the association as required by the regulations and there you go. Add more professional organizers, or not, as long as there is content and looks relevant you have created instance expert status upon yourself.

Testimonials should always be a part of your guerrilla marketing plan. A lot of people will go to great lengths to find people to write a testimonial. However, most people are too busy either to write one, take forever to get to writing it or forget about your request. We rarely ask them a second time to write a testimonial and it's our loss.

One trick I have learned is to write my own testimonial to address the issue I want to stress. If I want service highlighted I will write a glowing 2 line testimonial saying how great I am.

Now don't fret it doesn't end there and no I am not being sneaky. I then go to a good client who is happy with my service, read them the quote I've written and ask them if I can ascribe the quote to them with their name and company below it. No one has ever declined a request like that.

Writing articles for the newspaper or other publication is another way to create a strong personal brand and have people look upon you as a leading expert, after you're published.

Articles are easier to write the ultimate authority creator, a book on the subject. I spoke to a friend recently who is on his second best seller book about business. He is revered around the country already, is asked to be an authority on TV news reports and, of course, is on the speaking tour making high 4 figure fees for expressing his views, which he has worked down into 5 different speeches he uses depending on the audience.

I'm taking a lesson from my friend as well. I asked him if I could write a monthly column on business for the national magazine he publishes. He knows me well and respects my opinions and gave me the green light. Next stop was to get his editor to help with the writing. Funny, I didn't ask if there was a payment for writing the column. Who cares, I'm getting what I want from it – another branding opportunity. I did get paid by the way.

I have been running for the Board of Directors of a very large financial institution for the last few years. A friend asked me why I would beat my head against the wall because I consistently come 20-30% below the last winning director. My profile and vision statement go out in a book form to 450,000 members with the voting package. If I don't get elected I still get visibility to all those people. More branding opportunities can always be created for sure. What have I got to lose?

Professionals such as lawyers will often give you 15 minutes of free advice. Of course, they are hoping you will hire them which can often happen. Try it yourself!

I think the days of high priced brochures are over for most businesses. Mind you, those big real estate projects may need those glossy brochures to entice people into their condo complexes but the average person doesn't need a brochure. I'm talking about the handyman, the accountant, the web master. Websites have replaced the Yellow Pages, the Business card and the brochure a long time ago. Blogs have replaced the website.

Your blog can be the ultimate marketing tool. Giving your opinions on important aspects of your business will bring people back to read more. The dynamic blog is above and beyond the business card type static website. Heck if you can't write from the heart on it, hire someone to write for you.

Social media – This is near and dear to my heart and the heart of my business. Take all the social media platforms and focus on Twitter to pull marketing to your blog, use Facebook to tell friends about specials, seminars and updates on your business and of course use LinkedIn to showcase your talents. The degree of success you will have is based on the level of engagement you have with your listening audience.

I love to engage people on Twitter, which is why I have well over 200,000 followers. I comment on a controversial topic and within minutes I have a debate going. It's fun and gets your name out there to the masses. I utilize pull marketing because I 'm not going to sell my followers anything. I do, however, want them to come to my blog so I tease them with a blog post I've written and watch the traffic come in – usually about 500 people drop by my blog within minutes of a post.

I was using a new tool lately, a video email system, TalkFusion which has multiple tools like video conferencing, tracking and others. There are many such programs out there so pick one that works for you. Google has a great service called Google Hangout which I like better.

Whatever you decide to do, bear in mind if you treat your customers like you want to be treated, (trite but true) you will get customers in time without a lot of expense and you will become a guerrilla marketer in the process.

SWOT Analysis

This SWOT isn't the elite cop, doesn't dress in black fatigues, carry a gun and assault criminals. A **SWOT** analysis is a tool for auditing an organization and its environment.

This is an important part of your marketing plan. You need to be able to identify the issues that will affect the success or failure of your business and have a realistic strategy to mitigate the problem areas.

SWOT means Strengths, Weaknesses, Opportunities and Threats. The first two are internal functions of the entrepreneur and the latter two are external forces affecting the company.

You define your personal Strengths and outline the advantages they give you to benefit the outcomes of the company. Your strengths will hopefully provide a focus from which you can build on.

You must then honestly identify your Weaknesses then figure out how you can mitigate those weaknesses. A good example of this is you have a great business opportunity and everything is in place except for the fact that you can't sell for beans and downright don't like sales.

What to do? To mitigate this weakness the normal person would hire a salesman; if you are weak in accounting hire a bookkeeper. You may need financing so you may need to mitigate your situation by bringing in a partner who does have money. I think you get the idea. Every problem has and needs a balancing positive aspect.

Opportunities are the external conditions that are helpful in achieving your corporate objectives. These are things which you have no control over so you better be prepared for them or at least identify them. Opportunities can be anything from a bad economy in which your product fills need to a new product developed to fill a niche.

In Vancouver during the 2009 recession, the opportunities were the 2010 Olympics in Whistler. In a poor economy, a recession proof product is an opportunity.

Threats are the scary external factors that can damage your business and like the weaknesses they need to be mitigated. I counseled a client who was trying to close a lease on a very desirable street in Vancouver for his coffee shop. As we negotiated the lease for the retail space the conditions became increasingly unfavourable to my client. I sensed something was afoot.

Sure enough the moment one of our meetings was canceled I realized Starbucks must be going after the same space. Boy was I right and in spades! My client lost the space to Starbucks who had correctly identified this demographic reach location as the best spot for their newest coffee shop.

My client's backup location was not a very good choice and against my advice he fell in love with the new location, opened quickly and failed just as quickly escaping into the night leaving his equipment for repossession.

Finding a Niche

Market niche defines the specific product features aimed at satisfying specific market needs, as well as the price range, production quality and the demographics that is intended to impact.

You need to fulfill a need with your business or you will be one of the milieu competing for sales. Create a unique niche and you will corner the market.

Carlsberg Beer decades ago opened a new niche in an uninspiring beer industry. They developed a beer that had 14% alcohol when normal beer was between 3.5-6% alcohol. It certainly became popular for a time.

A friend of mine brought the first bungee jump concept to Canada years ago. He had successfully found an undiscovered niche in the adventure industry. No one had a clue what this new adventure was but was enamored by it for sure. His niche was replicated over and over again and he made a lot of money.

You need to find a missing link, a new function for an old product, or an undiscovered way to earn revenue. The internet is the new frontier in this respect and has made millionaires from niche marketing.

Corporate Intelligence

Go ask for some help from someone outside Your Geographic Area.

What's that you say? That sounds goofy and why would someone help you with your company? People are generally generous with information and you will find a lot of people just love to talk about themselves and their businesses.

Many years ago, at a time when every corner had a video store renting Betamax and VHS video tapes (if you remember back that far) I had a client who needed help setting up his business. I had lots of ideas how to market a video store but no clue as to the numbers of videos one needed to stock, how to determine the titles a person must order and how to setup a control system for signing titles out to customers. What to do?

I went through the Yellow Pages from Kelowna, a town about 300 miles from Vancouver and found a video store just like the one my client wanted to open and operate. I called and asked to speak to the owner who luckily answered the phone. He was the owner/operator, manager, janitor and bookkeeper and was very pleasant on the phone.

I told him our dilemma and we spoke for 2 hours about my client and all the ins and outs of the operation. Why would he be so open to me he didn't have a clue who I was representing? When I chose a video owner to call I picked a location with the same demographics as my client and to whom I was not direct competition because of distance.

I quite liked the gentleman from Kelowna. He had been running his little shop successfully for several years and was close to retirement. He had several full and part time staff as well as a wealth of information for my client. He liked to work the odd shift because he liked the personal interaction with his customers. I offered him a deal!

I invited to pay for him and his wife to come to Vancouver at our expense to help my client in person. I also offered to pay him $500 a day for as long as he wanted to stay. It didn't hurt to ask. He jumped at the deal, a mini holiday and some cash for his expertise. We got a lot more than our money's worth from this fellow. My client went on to run a very successful little video store. He had already moved on by the time the big box video stores like Blockbuster came on the scene and put all the corner stores including his old store out of business.

A general in China once wrote a book in BCE (that's before Christ) about the strategies used in winning a battle and therefore the war. The book, the Art of War, by General Sun Tsu wasn't a bestseller at the time but today his theories of warfare are taught at the LSE (London School of Economics) and at Harvard Business School.

Why teach the warfare strategies of a 4000 year old dead general to business students? His war strategies can be used in a business marketing environment just as easily in our time as it was successful in war in his time.

When you read the following tactics imagine that Chinese General and how doing business, especially in a bad economy is like going to do battle for life or death.

The General's five most desired traits equate to those of a successful entrepreneur.

Wisdom is the quality of being able to make sound, logical decisions. It doesn't come easy and can only be perfected through years of study and experience.

Credibility is being able to gain the trust of others through dependable and consistent demeanour. As such, little effort is needed to 'rally the troops'.

<u>Benevolence</u> means the intentions of the businessman are always focused on being concerned for his employee's well-being.

The entrepreneur's <u>Courage</u> is one of his most valuable traits, without which he cannot effectively lead. He is self confident in knowing that as he leads others will follow. Doubt Kills the Warrior!

<u>Discipline</u> prevents him from growing soft. I keep a notepad next to my bed at night in case I awake with some transitory thought about my business that I need to write down. An entrepreneur must be alert to opportunity and be ready for it. His standards are high and kept high.

Sun Tzu urges the Warrior (Entrepreneur) to examine the situation, and most particular, the advantages.

Leverage those advantages to the fullest.

The entrepreneur has to get his ducks in a row, so to speak, prior to starting his business or initiating a new strategy in an existing business. This means taking steps in advance to give you the best chance possible of achieving success.

Looking at this from a business perspective, if you are going to run a company, there are both initial start up costs and ongoing expenses which must be accounted for.

The Dot-com crash of 1999 was a pretty good example of what can happen when people forget this.

"Therefore those skilled in warfare move the enemy, and are not moved by the enemy."-Sun-Tzu.

This is a very important quote. Basically what this means is that the entrepreneur's competition must play by your game, not you by his game.

This is simply saying that the first to market has the advantage and that the competition wanting to follow is at a big disadvantage.

Doing the right things at the right times

An entrepreneur should surround himself with skilled managers and trained employees. A small company should be careful when coming up against a giant competitor. Invincibility results from doing the right things at the right times.

During the 1970s, Digital Equipment Co. (DEC) in Massachusetts ceded the mainframe computer business to IBM and focused on developing and marketing their line of mini-computers. DEC exploited IBM's absence from the marketplace and from 1972-1985 they had phenomenal success. DEC eventually became Digital and was acquired by HP. Millions was made by all.

Watch out for Wal-Mart. They are exploiting their core competencies in technology and inventory management and transferring those skill sets by building bigger stores that offers far more goods than the classical Wal-Mart store from 10-15 years ago. At the same time, Wal-Mart has excelled in exploiting their economies of scale and is the major reason why stores like K-Mart have very little time left before they go belly-up.

Weakness and Strength

In business, perceiving one's environment, maintaining flexibility and adaptability are keys to success. You must know your strengths and weaknesses as well as perform a SWOT analysis as part of your Business Plan (SWOT is Strengths, Weaknesses, Opportunities and Threats). One must always be prepared to seize the initiative when an opportunity presents itself. Carpe Diem!

Armed Struggle

"One, who does not know the mountains and forests, gorges and defiles, swamps and wetlands cannot advance the army. One who does not use local guides cannot take advantage of the ground."-Sun-Tzu.

You as a business person must know 'the lay of the land' when going out for business. This mitigates the disadvantages of facing the competition.

Principles of warfare

Do not depend on the enemy (competitor) not coming, but depend on your readiness against him. Do not depend on the competition to keep a distance but depend on your business being prepared when they do come.

Do not attempt the insane – like setting up a coffee shop next to Starbucks. Join forces with like-minded businesses or setup strategic alliances. Starbucks has been opening stores in unusual spaces in the past few years like Grocery stores and even churches. Do not leave yourself open to attacks from your competition. Be prepared. If you are going to go after your competitors go there to beat them – take no prisoners.

Strategic Planning, the General has to have a plan of attack

An entrepreneur who lacks strategic planning and doesn't work with a Business Plan will fail. If the entrepreneur gives out rewards frequently, he is running out of resources.

The Battle Field

It's not a question of winning the battle; it's a question of how you win. Because how you win proves that you are either a great strategist or a bad one. If everything is in your favour and you fail, it's your skill as an entrepreneur that caused the failure

Unpredictability has won many battles

Be unpredictable. With good strategies and intelligence (the military kind) you can pick the time to go after your competition and hit them with surprise.

Using Spies for intelligence

Gathering data is one step. Interpreting it is another. I get my clients to call or visit the competition and see how they do business, what they charge for products or services and generally find weaknesses and strengths in order to run their business better and to better compete. You can get friends to help you if you feel being a 'spy' is not for you.

Types of Marketing from Viral to Engagement

Marketers are always coming up with innovative methods to sell products and services. There are general principles to marketing but much of it is based on the psychology of sales as well as the behaviours and experiences of the consumer.

<u>Engagement marketing</u> is the most recent manner of marketing and refers to the Social Media phenomenon of the last few years. It specifically refers to engagement of the consumer to help market the product or service on behalf of the business selling it.

In social media terms using Twitter I 'tweet' about my business in 140 characters or letters and my 'followers' will RT or retweet my message to their followers. A simple message can in a matter of seconds be let loose on hundreds of thousands of viewers who refer the business to others. Facebook does the same engagement in a smaller less immediate format.

<u>Viral Marketing</u> is like the video of Susan Boyle that was on YouTube and went from thousands to multi-millions of viewers in days. I tell two friends and they tell two friends. It's like that question would you take a million bucks or two cents doubled every day for a month. Well we all know that two cents doubled every day works out to about $3 million bucks.

<u>Buzz Marketing</u> literally refers to creating a buzz for the product. Vespa scooters did an unusual marketing program some time ago in NYC. They gave 50 gorgeous models the high end scooters and told them to have coffee all day at Starbucks across the city and of course to make sure they parked their Vespa next to them on the sidewalk next to the patio where they sat. People noticed both the model and the scooter.

When RIM (now Blackberry); the Canadian makers of Blackberry, were doing their market research they gave 300 of the first batch of devices to a select group of high end CEO's and Ad agency types on a 3 month trial. After the three month trial period they tried to take them away from the executives. No Way Jose!! Those ad guys were hooked on the little Blackberry.

Relationship Marketing has been used by car salesman for decades. Make the 'mark', excuse me.. the customer, your 'buddy' and keep in touch with them by phone or mail every few months so the customer will be reminded of your caring thoughtfulness when a new car purchase is anticipated or when the newest model is released.

Guerrilla Marketing does not involve a big ape rather it is based on the militia type guy sneaking out of the bushes and capturing you - or in this case your attention. Guerrilla marketing relies on a lot of imagination, time and hard work versus a big budget. The term was coined and defined by Jay Conrad Levinson in his book *Guerrilla Marketing*.

A fellow photographer buddy moved to Vancouver from a large market in the states and wanted to market himself to the elite of Vancouver's ad agency niche.

He had spent lots of money on his move and his new studio so the marketing budget was small and he needed to make a splash.

His office was on a third floor walk-up downtown. He brought in 5 tons of dirt and created a sandy beach with lots of lighting, umbrella and fake water in his studio. He sent the invitations out to all the people he wanted to meet written on a Frisbee which included a drink coupon and suntan lotion and a couple of other novelty items. A lot of people showed up for his beach party since the weather outside was very cold (February) and they were curious. He made a lot of friends that day and more importantly future clients were shown his creativity.

All of the above marketing campaigns form a portion of a comprehensive marketing plan. Wikipedia notes the following types of marketing that people have used in the past. As you can see they can be very specific. So next time someone lumps Marketing in with sales you can tell them marketing is a complex way of getting your message out to the masses. Remember how you got to be reading this, was it affiliate, buzz, viral, engagement, ambush marketing or something else or a hybrid of all of them?

Types of Marketing according to Wikipedia:

Ambush marketing is a marketing strategy wherein the advertisers associate themselves with, and therefore capitalize on, a particular event without paying any sponsorship fee.

Buzz marketing. The term "buzz marketing" originally referred to oral communication but in the age of Web 2.0, social media such as Facebook and Twitter are also being used to create marketing buzz.

Cause marketing. This refers to a type of marketing involving the cooperative efforts of a for-profit business and a non-profit organization for mutual benefit. The term is sometimes used more broadly and generally to refer to any type of marketing effort for social and other charitable causes, including in-house marketing efforts by non-profit organizations. Cause marketing differs from corporate giving (philanthropy) as the latter generally involves a specific donation that is tax deductible, while cause marketing is a marketing relationship not necessarily based on a donation.

Communal marketing. This term is generally used to refer to sponsored content on blogs, wikis, forums, social networking web sites and individual Web sites.

Community marketing. This is a strategy to engage an audience in an active, non-intrusive prospect and customer conversations.

Cross-media marketing. This is a form of cross-promotion in which promotional companies commit to surpassing the traditional advertisements and decide to include extra appeals to their offered products.

Customer advocacy. This is a specialized form of customer service in which companies focus on what is best for the customer.

Database marketing. This is a form of direct marketing using databases of customers or potential customers to generate personalized communications in order to promote a product or service for marketing purposes.

Digital marketing. This is marketing that makes use of electronic devices such as computers, tablets, smart-phones, cell phones, digital billboards, and game consoles to engage with consumers and other business partners. Internet Marketing is a major component of digital marketing.

Direct marketing. This is a channel-agnostic form of advertising that allows businesses and non-profit organizations to communicate straight to the customer, with advertising techniques that can include Smart-phone text messaging, apps, email, interactive consumer websites, on-line display ads, fliers, catalog distribution, promotional letters, and outdoor advertising.

Diversity marketing. This is a marketing paradigm which sees marketing (and especially marketing communications) as essentially an effort in communication with diverse publics. According to the paradigm, the main focus of marketing today should be to create effective communication methods and a communication mix appropriate to each of the diverse group's active in the market.

Ethical marketing. The increasing trend of **fair trade** is an example of the impact of ethical marketing.

Evangelism marketing. This is an advanced form of word-of-mouth marketing (WOMM) in which companies develop customers who believe so strongly in a particular product or service that they freely try to convince others to buy and use it. The customers become voluntary advocates, actively spreading the word on behalf of the company.

Global marketing. This is "marketing on a worldwide scale reconciling or taking commercial advantage of global operational differences, similarities and opportunities in order to meet global objectives".

Inbound marketing. This is advertising a company through blogs, podcasts, video, eBooks, eNewsletters, white papers, SEO, social media marketing, and other forms of content marketing.

Influencer marketing. This is a form of marketing that has emerged from a variety of recent practices and studies, in which focus is placed on specific key individuals (or types of individual) rather than the target market as a whole. It identifies the individuals that have influence over potential buyers, and orients marketing activities around these influencers.

Internet marketing. Also known as *online advertisement, internet marketing, online marketing* or *e-marketing*, is the marketing and promotion of products or services over the Internet.

Loyalty marketing. This is an approach to marketing, based on strategic management, in which a company focuses on growing and retaining existing customers through incentives.

Multi-level marketing (MLM) or Network marketing. This is a marketing strategy in which the sales force is compensated not only for sales they personally generate, but also for the sales of the other salespeople that they recruit.

Nano-campaigning. This refers to an approach within Marketing communications, Public relations and Lobbying which uses personalized and product-specific or issue-specific tactics as the starting point for more extensive strategic campaigns.

Next best action marketing. As a special case of next-best-action decision-making, is a customer-centric marketing paradigm that considers the different actions that can be taken for a specific customer and decides on the 'best' one.

Permission marketing. Marketers obtain permission before advancing to the next step in the purchasing process. For example, they ask permission to send email newsletters to prospective customers.

Proximity marketing. This is the localized wireless distribution of advertising content associated with a particular place.

Transparent Marketing. This is a strategy used to personalize the content marketed to a customer by engaging them in Web 2.0 social media technologies such as blogs, live chat and product ratings.

Undercover marketing. (Also known as buzz marketing, *stealth marketing*, or by its detractors *roach baiting*) is a subset of guerrilla marketing where consumers do not realize they are being marketed to. For example, a company might pay an actor or socially adept person to use a certain product visibly and convincingly in locations where target consumers congregate.

Strategic Alliances.

Strategic Alliances are about as complicated as the name; two parties getting together for mutual benefit. Your marriage can be called a strategic alliance for sure but in these terms we are talking about business.

My clients include suppliers who have offered preferred buying status to my clients but it typically includes a mutual benefit that may or may not be a seller/buyer relationship.

Imagine two stores side by side on a street, one sells pencils and the other sells pencil cases (using the simplest example). Wouldn't it be beneficial for both to offer sales based on the combination or combine their advertising budgets so they can mutually benefit from the synergistic sale?

A strategic alliance can exist for a number of reasons in terms of products, distribution channels, manufacturing capability, expertise, project funding, capital equipment, knowledge, or intellectual property. An example of the latter would be the bundling of software with the purchase of a computer or operating system. Think of the benefits both parties could reap from such an arrangement.

My buddy **Gordon Ross** owned Net Nanny, the first software to protect children on the internet. He went right to Bill Gates and suggested Microsoft 'bundle' his new software with each Windows operating system Microsoft sold. Gates was impressed and a strategic alliance was born.

The Strategic Alliance can be very loosely set up like the two store example or where advice is shared to a very complex business alliance called a Joint Venture where one company enters into a contractual basis with another company for mutual benefit including shared expenses and reduced risk.

Some Strategic alliances can be done with a handshake or a complex agreement.

Some ways to connect in a strategic alliance relationship:

Partner with a former employer

Partner with a competitor

Cross sector partnerships

Partner with a brand leader

Partner with a key customer

Partner for cross marketing

You started your business as a one man show but sometimes it's fun and profitable to share resources, risks and profits.

Tips on Direct Marketing

Direct marketing is a straight to the customer form of marketing.

The thing about going directly to the customer is that you can measure results of your marketing faster and easier. Things like couponing, telemarketing, direct response TV ads, landing pages and aWeber broadcast emails can all be tracked with little effort.

The good part about measurable Return on Investment (ROI) is that you can change the marketing method immediately if the campaign isn't working. Do you think Edison invented the modern light bulb on the first try? Edison said "I have not failed. I've just found 10,000 ways that won't work." He learned something from each iteration which brought him closer to his goal. If you're not making lots of mistakes, you're not learning anything.

People can generally be fooled about the way they perceive money and value. It's not trickery it's just how the mind works. When you manage your campaign you have to test not just prices, but price presentations. Consider when buying a magazine subscription, would you rather pay $24 per year or $2 per issue? How about $14.95 or $15? My favorite, of course, is the price you pay at the gas pump. I'd like to see someone try to buy a gallon of gas with a tenth of a cent. This concept of taking off a nickel or a cent to the lower price originated in the 1950's and was designed to psychologically make the price seem lower. I've actually experimented with this and the lower price even by a cent makes people purchase the item.

Sometimes things just don't go the way you plan. A test flops. Sales fall. And you just can't explain it. Usually it's temporary. The point is, don't panic and change your entire marketing strategy based on short-term results. And never, ever discard a control until you have something that tests better.

Never confuse activity with progress. You need to map out a measurable strategy before launching any marketing campaign. And you need to execute your strategy carefully and methodically. If all you're doing is slapping together one ad after another, you'll get nowhere fast.

I recently did a global product launch for a client. We realized we had 'too many cooks in the kitchen' and had to create protocols to measure change more accurately. You see the problem was we would change the format on the online sales page, as well as strategic placement of the price of the product plus a couple of other changes. After the changes we measured increase or decrease in the sale of the product. Unfortunately, when change was evident, we couldn't tell which activity accounted for the change. What was the solution? Make one significant change then wait 2 days and measure the difference.

Still with the global launch scenario our stats proved that when you get right down to it, it's like an envelope. An envelope is nothing more than a container for printed matter after all. It carries your message to the destination and then gets ripped open. Your marketing piece or web page can be a four-color design masterpiece, but it doesn't have to be. Many times a plain old #10 is all you need.

I'm forever amazed at how little thought people put into the creative process. Personally, I spend at least half of any given project on gathering information and brainstorming. When you think things through first, copy and design are a lot easier and usually far more successful.

I think by now all of us have encountered those annoying 'landing pages' marketers are so fond of using to sell a product or service online. Your customers know the difference between BS and information. So don't try to shovel a pile of one to cover up for a lack of the other. Give details. Answer questions and objections. Provide a means for customers to easily find out more (a web site is good for this.) People often make buying decisions based on a single feature.

Look at the numbers. Do surveys. Run focus groups. Talk to your customers. Your customers will tell you everything you need to know if you just open your eyes and ears.

As the famous baseball Catcher Yogi Bera once said, *"It ain't over till it's over."* You can guess, estimate, reason and calculate, but you really don't know anything until you run a test. If there's one thing that's for sure in this business, it's that nothing is for sure.

Chapter Seven

Engaging Your Clients

Social Media Marketing, the New Standard

1) Why Do You THINK You Need A Social Media Strategy?

Sounds like a silly question to some but if you if don't understand social media, don't know how to do it or can't comprehend its relevance or don't even care then maybe it's not for you. Remember you can always get someone to take care of it for you. I tend to think anyone not working on a social media package is out of the loop. Your business will continue to run poorly and it's a matter of time before you and your business will be out of business.

So, assuming you understand social media and its relevance in the new world order what are your goals? Do you want greater sales conversions? Increased traffic to your website? Or would you like greater brand awareness? Each of these questions uncovers a unique set of behaviours necessary to achieve your goal.

2) Identify Which Platforms Are Right For You

I'm pretty sure every business owner knows who his target market is and how to convince them to buy their product or service. But knowing your demographics may only confuse you when you are looking at spending time and/or money on social media platforms.

What are Platforms? I'm not trying to be techno here but this is the social media that is appropriate to your business, your style and you customer demographic. I'm talking about Twitter, FaceBook, and LinkedIn to start. First break down the demographic makeup of your potential customer base. This will allow you to identify the appropriate channels for your social media campaign. How? If your primary focus is business-to-consumer interactions, you may focus more on integrating Facebook and Twitter into your strategy. However, if you service other businesses, LinkedIn will likely be your primary tool of choice because of its' business orientation versus a social one.

3) Create Brand Awareness

You need to develop an 'image' of yourself and your business or at least have it in some sort of strategy before you can expect to utilize all the social media well. Create a blog for yourself because it is dynamic versus a laid pack old web page.

Change your content regularly.

Optimize your logo and graphic to load fast on your blog. No one waits anymore!

Get a great picture for your Twitter account and create a cool background to put it on.

Send newsletters out to prospective customers and existing customers; add links to every one of the newsletters and emails you send.

Secure your own domain every which way to Sunday because trust me getting domain names is tough. I've sold one for $30,000 and lost one because I failed to renew in time. That was worth a lot more.

4) Develop a Social Media Process Plan

Whether you do your own social media or have someone else you need a plan. Check out my free 33 Point Checklist on Social Media first then go from there (in the Appendix). This document will serve as your standard operating procedure for social media engagement.

Get someone to initially help you set up a plan that suits you. Set up procedures that will make social media fun not laborious. Set usual times to send stuff out or use great products like Hootsuite to automate timing.

If you have staff willing to help, allocate specific tasks and or days to work on social media. One of my clients gave all of his staff iPhones and insisted they tweet 10 times a day to customers about the business. Provide training to these staff.

Be very clear how you will measure your ROI (Return on Investment -there are tools) and what you expect to get from it. Besides possible customers my main goal is to get my name and message out to entrepreneurs struggling with all this social media stuff.

5) Understand SEO (Search Engine Optimization)

Whatever you do, don't launch your social media campaign without obtaining at least a basic understanding of SEO. Knowing how to increase your chances of being found on the internet is essential for increased online traffic and target market conversion! Wordpress, my blogging platform (there's that word again) has 'plug ins' that make SEO very easy. You just need to input key words into your blog relating to your business and blog topic.

6) Create a Social Media Policy

I'm keen on this if you are running a bigger company and having others post tweets and write for you be it a blog or on Facebook. Are employees allowed to post to their personal social media accounts during work hours? Who is responsible for monitoring the communications of the social media team? Or, if an employee encounters an unhappy customer, is there a protocol for off line follow-up?

Take these 6 steps seriously and remember if you work ON your business not IN it you don't need to be the social media guru, you just need to find someone who is and hire them.

Since Social media is becoming the norm it takes us away from direct contact with those who we really want to impact – new customers. While Social media reaches so many more people there is nothing like grasping the hand of a new contact, looking him in the eye and making a connection.

Engagement Marketing & Social Media Networking

Relationship Marketing focuses on keeping clients rather than trying to acquire customers like other traditional marketing methods. You'll get the usual 6 month call from your favorite car dealer asking you if you are 'satisfied' with your car and by the way would you like a new one. Keep the customer happy

Then fast forward to Engagement Marketing. In Internet terms it would the equivalent of Web 4.0

*"**Engagement marketing**, sometimes called experiential marketing, event marketing, live marketing or "participation marketing," is a marketing strategy that directly engages consumers and invites and encourages consumers to participate in the evolution of a brand. Rather than looking at consumers as passive receivers of messages, engagement marketers believe that consumers should be actively involved in the production and co-creation of marketing programs." - Wikipedia*

When consumers actually engage with a brand and share that experience with friends and family, social media platforms accelerate and broaden that sharing exponentially. So you can see how important Social media like Twitter (even though it doesn't have a business model) is to the development of brand marketing.

People are social animals and we all have the need to communicate. How can anyone explain the power of Twitter and before that Facebook? The immediacy of Twitter takes it one step higher, faster, and further than Facebook.

Inbound vs. Outbound Marketing

It's not hard to see the Internet as a two way street, you engage with people and they respond like a conversation. Traditional methods of marketing are rarely effective on the Internet. I used to be a Cracker Jack marketing guy, I used to be a lot of things a few years ago, but in today's fast and immediate Internet world traditional marketing is out the window.

We call the marketing landscape one of two things, Inbound (pull) or Outbound (Push) marketing. You be the judge of what would be more effective for your business.

Inbound Marketing (Pull Marketing)

Customers are interactive between yourself and them.

Marketers provide more benefits and value to the prospective customer because there is so much free stuff out there on the net. They almost need to keep people engaged, educated and entertained. Prospective customers come to you through referrals, affiliates and search engines.

Outbound Marketing (Push Marketing)

Communication is pushed upon your prospective customer. You give them an ad or a brochure but there is little of value coming from you; just the hope people will buy from you.
You don't educate, engage or entertain people.

Those poor Out-bounders are facing some tough statistics. Hundreds of millions of people in Canada and the US have registered their phone numbers on a 'Do Not Call' list; people turn off and go fix a snack when TV ads come on during their favourite TV show. Half of all direct mail that comes to your home is unopened, and people who find ads coming up on their favourite website actually opt-out once the ads come up. (Watch out Facebook).

One of my consultants told me marketing as we know it will be obsolete in 10 years; I suggested two years was more to the point. As it turned out I was right.

Who has a Yellow Page ad, a printed brochure or a flyer? We now have QR codes on the back of a business card pulling us to a hot website or pdf of a brochure, because the old ways of getting your attention is gone. Mind you I have a plumber friend who pays $9000 a month for a double page Yellow Page ad, pays $4000/month for a TV spot and has trucks loaded with advertising. He won't change because these tools have been in place so long people actually find it a convenient way to find his services.

Inbound Marketers base their success on loyalty and do so after gaining your trust. I collect emails as an opt-in practice by giving people a free eBook about Social Media Networking, having had over 200,000 followers on Twitter I know a little about that. Now mix in videos (which any fool can make and edit in minutes on their net book), blogs, pod casts, info-graphics and white papers and everyone has become an expert in a given field. Read Millionaire Messenger by Brendan Burchard for further information.

It's all about content, CRM, Social media, engagement. If you give people something interesting in any of the pull marketing strategies people will be more apt to buy from you. Don't forget about all those friends and others who see your marketing piece and send it out to their associates and their own friends. I have well over 4000 people following me on LinkedIn who have a combined influence over 23 million others, on Twitter my influence is over 50 million.

Unlike Vegas, where everything done in Vegas stays in Vegas, everything you say and do on the internet stays on it forever. Your marketing efforts do as well and a good idea will go viral. I sometimes get a little overwhelmed on the internet when it comes to the newest and best marketing methods. I'd suggest to you that adding one strategy at a time and getting good at it before adding another strategy might be the best way to enter social media marketing. Don't let it intimidate you!

Now that you obviously understand all the nuances of traditional marketing and inbound versus outbound marketing you will also understand that the next step is to realize that the future of marketing is inbound marketing. Let's explore that a little further.

Raise Your Game, Entrepreneurs – Social Media/Inbound Marketing

The time to experiment with Social Media is past, it is not going away and if your business is not heavily involved in a Social Media campaign you will lose to your competition.

Large corporations are now devoting a significant budget in terms of human resources and money to making the most of their brand with social media and getting rid of their expenses and outdated advertising campaigns.

Inbound Marketing (or providing customer content) like Blogs, YouTube, pod casts, video, eBooks, eNewsletters, white papers, SEO, social media marketing, has taken the place of the Outbound

Marketing (buying customer's attention) which we have always considered traditional marketing, e.g. brochure, cold calling, flyers, billboards, direct mail, radio and TV.

Social Media is inexpensive, relevant, and easy to implement. The barrier to entry no longer exists. Your social media must cover the following four objectives.

Positioning. Synchronize your objectives, both business and social.

Outcome Maximize results by allocating social media where and when it makes sense in your marketing plan.

Systems Integration. Create a system that makes all your actions run smoothly

Client Engagement. Strengthen the core of your social media success rather than being left behind by the competition.

There is still a need, maybe more so, for the human connection and the following will give you some insight into handling and managing the art of personal networking one on one.

Since Social media is becoming the norm it takes us away from direct contact with those who we really want to impact – new customers. While Social media reaches so many more people there is nothing like grasping the hand of a new contact, looking him in the eye and making a connection.

Comparing Social Media

I've had a business website since 1993 yet I struggled with the idea that I needed to upgrade my tired old website to a Web 2.0 blog. I'd say most businesses are switching their corporate website to more of a social networking site utilizing a blog format changing the tired static website to a dynamic blog.

Wordpress (the number one blog open source software) is the choice for most or typical social media software. Fortune Magazine says that 46% of the Fortune 500 has a corporate blog. I'm surprised the number is not higher. I think Vancouver is on the leading edge of this trend as I know a great many large companies which not only blog but use Twitter as an Engagement marketing tool.

Social Networking has increased exponentially particularly on Twitter. In a recent survey among my clients 8 in 10 had twitter accounts. This is significant from a year ago when none of them had accounts.

MySpace appeals to a young demographic. It has become a great marketing site for musicians and artists. It's mainly a source of video content. Music videos and ads tend to go viral like YouTube.

YouTube tends to be a topic oriented website versus a network oriented one. Businesses are very visible on the web and ads are very apropos as well as expected on there. I like the fact you can see your favourite music video or find an instruction video on how to play lead guitar or pickle beets.

Google has embraced this marketing tool and has placed considerable weight on it for searchable content. Your business media must include YouTube as an option.

Facebook reminds me of the grad book in my old high school. It brings old friends together; existing friends become tighter and invites new friends to join a close knit network. There are lots of applications to make Facebook an all encompassing experience. Facebook appeals to an older demographic meaning 35-60 yrs. Facebook tends to be highly personal if one is inclined that way but most shy away from giving out too much information. I like to use mine for business without a lot of really personal information. An amusing story the other day stated that the youth are leaving Facebook because they don't want their parents and grandparents to read what they are up to.

LinkedIn.com is a career and business oriented social networking site. It's very much like Facebook in that it gathers like-minded individuals but it differs in that its focus is on business, career and networking. I secured a major client (a foreign government) from my profile on LinkedIn. LinkedIn is a source of fodder for Recruiters and Head Hunters seeking the new CEO of that new media corporation. LinkedIn is strongly targeted to business versus a friend-type database.

Twitter.com I enjoy my Twitter because it is so dynamic. You get spontaneous 'tweets' about silliness and tweets about profundities. It's fun; filled full of ads like the old days on websites, innovative, did I say fun and since the tweets must be so short at 140 characters, you learn to be very frugal in your writing style. The marketing aspect is huge. As you gain 'followers' you then become eligible for pay per tweet status and might even make some money doing what is fun.

Meetup.com. According to Wikipedia **Meetup.com** (also called **Meetup**) is an online social networking portal that facilitates offline group meetings in various localities around the world. Meetup allows members to find and join groups unified by a common interest, such as politics, books, games, movies, health, pets, careers or hobbies. This phenomenon is incredible for linking up like-minded people in any number of locales for personal or business.

Social Media Reputation Management

FLASH - a Young man, a hero, standing up for someone on a bus was brutally murdered, the alleged perpetrator was described as black, 6'2", with curly black hair, hardly a great description. One man, a father of 2 young children, was immediately identified as the 'murderer' and people threatened him on Facebook then suggested others should 'viral' this guy's face and stats. He lost his job, threatened with death and vilified.

The problem? – The police immediately ruled him out as a suspect. He was playing cards miles away with friends.

The point? In a heartbeat this innocent man's reputation and life was destroyed by social media vigilantes. Once something about you hits the web it is impossible to retrieve it and delete that which has been said to the world. Yikes!

Social media has created a situation whereby a person or brand can be elevated substantially, quickly an also, destroyed in a heartbeat. Search engines and social media websites create a forum where anything can be said about you with little or no moderation.

We're learning of course, from changing privacy settings, to customizing who can see our profiles and posts from keeping very personal information off websites to monitoring pictures released or 'tagged' on Facebook. I don't want a picture of me at a college party from 30 years ago posted online to embarrass me, there's got to be a couple. One big thing I've learned is not to email, or post information after having a glass of chardonnay (my fav) – the Chardonnay Effect! Save the email and mail it the next day.

According to the Pew Research Center 57% of users check out their own names on the internet to see what is being said about them, about 46% check out others on the internet. I think it's a lot higher than that.

You can monitor yourself on the internet. Setup alerts with Google to see where your name comes up, do a search of your name on a regular basis and use a monitoring tool like Radian6.

If you are monitoring your brand and company develop a policy for immediate response to negative publicity, I respond immediately and with humility, this is not the time to be defensive.

Remember, after all is said and done, your reputation is your most valuable asset – Protect it!

Chapter Eight

No Sales No Business

Confidence to Sell Your Product

Repeating Yourself Too Much

Using Too Much Jargon

Not Being Consistent

Failing to Incorporate Feedback

Taking Too Many Perspectives Into Account

Failing to Acknowledge the Competition

Writing a business plan is often a crucial first step to getting your start-up off the ground. A good plan can help you raise money, recruit members of your management team, set your marketing strategy and, perhaps best of all, refine your thinking. A plan riddled with errors? That can sink you. Here are 10 mistakes that entrepreneurs frequently make when crafting their business plans, according to Akira Hirai, a consultant in California who advises start-up companies on elements of business-plan writing, including competitive analysis and financial forecasting.

You cannot expect a business plan to appeal to every possible audience. With this in mind, try to pick one business model, and focus on one industry or one problem. Otherwise, you risk spreading yourself too thin, and potentially creating a sprawling plan that makes a bad first impression.

It's a terrible sign if a potential client gets two pages into your plan and is bored. It is important to have the reader interested right from the executive summary on the very first page. And don't neglect your cover page: a well-designed logo never hurts.

Although it may seem impressive if you project vast markets and the potential for huge sums of revenue, outsize financial estimates often appear gimmicky to investors. Worse, big numbers often make you sound as if you don't know what you're doing or how hard it will be to penetrate your target market. Don't make big promises unless you're absolutely sure you can keep them.

In an effort to portray confidence, too many business plans ignore the competition that a new business will face. Ignoring the competition betrays a lack of sophistication, because most people have a fear and face the inevitable lack of confidence.

Pricing Your Product or Service

Pricing your products or service is a strategic tool, even a weapon in a good marketer's hand. Pricing will make or break your business in a heartbeat. Imagine not knowing your costs and selling a large inventory of product three times cheaper than the total cost of selling them- ouch! You'd be out of business on your first big sale.

There are a few things you need to take care of price-wise as part of your Strategic Marketing plan.

Set a goal for each sale. Your price will be determined by your overall marketing strategy and how you want to position that product or service. Let's say you have a product to sell – a widget. Do you want large numbers of customers or a few with a higher price? A classic case is selling a widget at $10 and selling a hundred or selling one widget at $1000. Which do you think would be easier to sell? The latter might be a luxury items like a Rolls Royce and the lesser product a Hyundai. The Rolls might be easier to sell in the right market.

Find Out What the Competition is Charging. In my blog about the Art of War, Sun Tsu suggested sending spies into the opposing army's camp to gather intelligence. The same works for business.

Pretend you want a job done or a product and call the competition. Getting your friends to do it is better for one simple reason. They won't know as much about the service as you and won't give your tactics away. One of the methods I like is to call the same business as you but in a completely different geographic location. What harm would it be for them to give you a little advice? Websites and journals etc may give you a hint of what the prevailing pricing may be for a product or service. Once you have found out the pricing range you can still alter the price higher or lower depending on your goals.

Determine Your Costs. You have to know your break-even point – the point where your costs match your sales. How much money do you need to bring in to be profitable? You will likely need to dig out your spreadsheet software and put <u>all</u> your expenses into it. Your expenses for your car, internet, business cards and those hidden ones you forget about like health care, an assistant when busy, etc.

Pricing. Selling a service? Are you going to bill by the hour (those clients who need you to hold their hand all the time will kill you) or by the project (if the hourly prices look like they might scare off the client)? Don't forget to take into account the down time (non-billable hours) needed to find the work you're getting paid to do.

I hope you have a Unique Selling Proposition (USP) or value added benefit to make you different from the other businesses in your industry. For example, your prices could be higher if you promise delivery of your work on a firm schedule, offer more experience than your competitors, or make a healthier food product.

Your Pricing Strategy. It's determined by your costs and your competition. Will you have one price for everyone or is it flexible? Are you going to sell wholesale and retail? Are you going to have discounted prices or maybe add something of value to the regular price as an incentive? Your distribution channels will affect your pricing, e.g. stores versus online.

Review your strategies frequently and be aware that <u>you can always make adjustments.</u>

Have you ever wondered if there was some reason behind a business pricing a product or service? Many books have been written about it and economists say there's a science behind it. Here are the top 15 pricing strategies:

Penetration Pricing – Low Price/High Volume, e.g. Wal-Mart

Market Skimming – High Price/ Low Volume, e.g. Tiffany's

Cost-Plus Pricing – Cost plus Mark-up, e.g. retail

Target Pricing – Target level of Profit, e.g. restaurants at 35%

Value Pricing- Price based on Consumer Perception, e.g. Mercedes

Loss Leader – Sold below cost to make sales elsewhere, e.g. IKEA hot dog & drink $1.50 in their store cafeteria.

Psychological Pricing – Significantly lower than reality, e.g. $9.99

Going Rate – Prices set following lead of rivals, e.g. gas stations

Tender Pricing – Bids for jobs, e.g. government

Marginal Cost Pricing – Set price in relation to Marginal Cost

Price Discrimination – Different price, same goods or service, e.g. online/store

Contribution Pricing – Variable/Direct Costs + Contribution to Fixed Assets

Absorption/Full cost Pricing – Set price to cover both Variable and Fixed costs, e.g. exporter

Influence of Elasticity – Inelastic, i.e. raise price if it doesn't make much difference /or Elastic, e.g. low computer prices= more buyers

...and my favourite

Predatory Pricing – This one kills the competition - Lower the price until you put the competition out of business.

Sales Funnel

New opportunities (or possible customer) are put in the top and worked through the funnel until they either issue a purchase order, or become a disqualified lead. The key to surviving in sales is to make sure that each layer never goes empty.

Sales funnel layers

New Opportunity
Initial Communication
Fact Finding
Develop Solution
Propose Solution
Solution Evaluation
Negotiation
Purchase Order
Account Maintenance

80/20 Rule

The 80/20 Rule means that in anything 20 percent are vital and 80 percent are trivial. In Italian economist Vilfredo Pareto's case it meant 20 percent of the people owned 80 percent of the wealth. In Quality Management pioneer, Dr. Joseph Juran's, initial work he identified 20 percent of the defects causing 80 percent of the problems.

Project Managers know that 20 percent of the work (the first 10 percent and the last 10 percent) consume 80 percent of your time and resources. You can apply the 80/20 Rule to almost anything, from the science of management to the physical world.

In sales, 80 percent of your sales will come from 20 percent of your customers and yes, unfortunately, you may have heard, 80% of your trouble in customer service comes from 20% of your customers.

Customer Service

Customer service is an important component of your business. I just became a patient of a new dentist closer to home. I was reassured by a personable receptionist and comforted by excellent care and dentistry. His easy-going demeanor and quality work made me smile. I figured his prices must be very high or at least on the high-end because of the well-appointed office and very professional work by him and his staff. I was pleasantly surprised to find out that the pricing was in the middle range but the service screamed expensive. A week later I received a nice little card thanking me for being a new client with a big smile. The large fridge magnet with a huge smile also helps keep my new dentist in my mind.

I recently referred a friend to an old client for some software work. I didn't expect anything, helping my friend was enough for me. About a week later I got a thank you note in the mail with a check for $100. Holy Moly, I called and told him I didn't want his money. He insisted and said he appreciated me thinking of him for work.

I'm amazed at how thoughtful people are, and to the extent people go to thank you for referrals, good work or well produced events, etc. I received a bottle of my favourite single malt scotch from one workshop participant. How she knew my liquor preference I've never figured out.

I tweeted about visiting my favourite coffee shop the other day to my 200,000 + Twitter followers and to my delight I got a gift certificate for a latte and a nice letter from the President of the coffee chain. The fact I know the President of the coffee chain shouldn't matter. He appreciated me thinking about him.

Giving advice about customer service is easy but often overlooked. There are several parameters necessary to make the most of the relationships between you and your customers.

Strive for the Best Quality

If some aspects of your business are suspect, or you are struggling with finance, HR, or whatever, as long as the quality of your product or service is high on your priority your customers will appreciate it and come back again and again. Trying to find new clients has a cost associated with it and if you can give them your best they will come back. The other issues will have to be dealt with but you will have a customer base.

Make Your Customer King

You need to continuously ask your customers for feedback. Consider issues that you would want addressed if you were the customer. Client feedback should be a welcome component of your sales cycle. You and your employees need to relish customer feedback so you can improve your product offering.

Quality and Prudent Staffing

I've seen start ups fill the employee ranks because they had the budget. A prudent entrepreneur keeps the HR lean and mean, fill as needed and never have excessive staffing. I always say, pay the most you can afford to those working with you and create an environment in which people will want to work for you. Paying your staff well reaps benefits for you because they will treat your customers better and have pride in their work.

Proactive Attitude

Running a business requires you to always be ahead of the game whether it's the competition or changing trends. You need to be a positive proactive thinker trying to be the go to guy/business for the latest or the greatest product or service. Always thinking of how to improve your customer's experience while they are in your care should be an ongoing concern.

Goal Priority

Any business person who doesn't write a business plan is a fool. The corollary to that being, if you have done a plan and fail to follow it you're an idiot, too. Goals don't have to be followed to the letter and can change as you grow but you need to know what the rules of the game are and where you need to be in a specific time line or you have nothing. Too many people consider themselves in the business plan without developing the plan with the customer in mind.

Ongoing SWOT Analysis

The cool part of being a small entrepreneur is being able to adapt quickly to market trends and competition jumping into your market. Developing a SWOT analysis (Strengths, Weaknesses,

Opportunities and Threats) and constantly monitoring it will help you keep on top of the competition. Keeping on top of the competition allows you to adapt immediately to possible trends. Take for instance you own a bar and your competition begins to offer entertainment where none existed. Analyzing what he's doing and figuring a better alternative will bode you well in the future.

Your Unique Selling Proposition (USP)

I assume you have a distinguishing product or service that makes you different from the competition. If you are just like the competition you will need to make up for the similarity with incredible customer service and better quality. I started going to a local eatery as a regular because they introduced themselves to me and remember my name. It reminds me of 'Cheers', "Where everybody knows your name". People want to feel accepted and important.

Effective Marketing

Your marketing doesn't have to cost you vast amounts of money to be effective. It does have to be targeted, be part of a strategy and must be cost effective to the money you have to spend. I can do a global launch with little spending compared to results. Effective marketing can be very 'guerrilla' if planned well in a systematic approach. I get all excited when I get a thank you email from a store who values my business. My optometrist sent me a birthday email with a printable voucher for $75 off my next pair of glasses. Of course, I'll be using her services again.

Understanding What Your Customer Needs

This may involve market research, polls, or something as simple as a gut feeling. The entrepreneur must understand the customer enough to know what the client needs. A restaurant patron may feel the food at his favourite eatery sucks and sets up his own restaurant to address the need for a quality wholesome food alternative. Typically businesses will come out of nowhere based on a perceived need for something missing or in an effort to create something better.

There is a fine line between running a great business and having a business that drives you into the ground because you've ignored customer service.

Chapter Nine
Managing What You've Got

Business Management

My team spends a lot of time introducing financial management to my clients. The biggest source of stress in any relationship, personal or business, is money and the lack thereof. If you have trouble handling money in your business you will lose both the money and your business.

You need to learn the basics of finance, either QuickBooks© or the industry standard Simply Accounting© software and then find yourself a good bookkeeper. Why learn QuickBooks if you still need a bookkeeper?

You need to understand where your money is going by being able to read a spreadsheet after your bookkeeper prepares it for you.

Make sure you open a business bank account rather than putting your business income in your personal account. The best reason is if you have a business name registered or not, your bank will not let you deposit a check in that name to your personal account, besides the IRS or Canada's CRA doesn't like you to mix business and personal funds in a bank account. It's called co-mingling.

I have a friend who hires a guy to mow his lawn, cleaners who clean his home, dry cleaners who pick up and deliver his clothes and a trainer that makes him work out twice a week in his home gym yet until recently he did his own company books.

Just to point out, he is good at his business, but not good with finances. Soon after he hired the bookkeeper and was told that he had more money than he thought he had - he was hooked. He's now happier, works on what he knows best and has more time to himself.

Building Your Dream Team for Your Business

CEO's, Consultants & Micro-Management

I want to talk about a group of consultants and, for the moment, let's say I was involved, working with a CEO as a client. It has changed my thoughts on coaching and has me thinking that perhaps a new model for my business needs to be planned.

Imagine a CEO running a large company to the point where he needs help but is reticent, no, maybe more worried, that his power will be usurped or worse he will lose total control of his company – his baby. Yikes, this sounds like the beginning of another EMyth lecture – not exactly.

Let's continue with this fictional company because it is a classic. Five new executives at the 'VP' level are brought in to take some of the stress off the CEO, give him more time to reflect on steady planned growth, allow him guidance on this planned growth and share his vision to these executives so all are on the same page.

Now there is a little more information to know here, Management Consultants secured the team and had gone in two months earlier to 'prime the operation' for change. This new team will report directly to the CEO and will be 'change agents' for him. The company having grown over 430% in the previous 3 years will now be poised to triple in size in the next year. That's the plan anyway.

What's the wild card here? You have 5 seasoned professionals, elite in their fields, seeing a bright future with this new company and having the belief that growth will move like lightning. The CEO is the wild card. You can't change a micro manager overnight just like a leopard can't change his spots. The management team believed they had turned around the CEO to believe change had to start at the top, that growth had reached a critical point where help was needed and that the potential was ripe for fast growth.

All the CEO saw was new faces, people he didn't scout or hire, who were undermining his authority, not allowing them to be bullied by him, and the ultimate for him; loss of control. In spite of the fact that he's a great guy, he couldn't see that listening to Consultants he brought in to work on a scenario that could explode in a positive way would be of benefit, and not to engage in a power struggle.

The team disintegrated in days. Dreams disappeared, questions arose, doubt entered minds, expertise was ignored and in the end the company was worse off than when the team came on board.

A positive, well-adjusted, experienced CEO needs to find employees, executives and consultant who can bring out the BEST in you. A CEO who looks for the worst will fail.

What failed in this business case? Did the CEO micro-manage senior executives used to running the show; yes. Maybe the team was too strong for the CEO to feel comfortable to manage effectively, could be. Was the team respected for their expertise? Not really or the CEO would have listened to them.

I think I will start a Project Management firm that will contract this type of scenario to more willing and open business owners. Then I can take on who I want to work with and who will bring out the best in me.

And yes, this was not fiction I was one of the five executives! I lasted 7 days.

I'll give some advice about people and the initial management styles needed to <u>work on</u> a business effectively and not <u>work in</u> it. Let's start with partnerships. Many people start them because they seem easier at the start, the attitude being that the other person can do all the work and 'I'll get rich', or the corollary to that is "I need the moral support of a partner because I'm afraid to do it myself".

A partnership needs to be like two hands interwoven. A partner great in sales would complement the other who liked working on the technical side of the business or liked doing a different aspect of the work. I was a partner in a commercial photography business years ago. My partner and I were both accomplished photographers so when work came in we fought over who was going to do it. One better suggestion would have been me partnering with a sales type. Oh well, live and learn and that's why I'm sharing my experience.

Employees - please don't hire your best friend because he is out of work and needs the job. It will come back to bite you when he really can't do the job you hired him for. You've heard the phrase don't lend friends money? Same thing! Another problem would be to hire family, it's OK to 'partner' with your wife but don't hire her, something about maintaining marital bliss!

Try to find the best employees for your money. I know a lot of you are saying, "Well, I really need a good expert but can only afford a junior marketing guy out of school." Consider incorporating if you haven't already and offer incentive shares of the business based on increased sales revenues, for instance, to the better marketing whiz. Sometimes I'll work for a client not because of the money but because it sounds cool, I like the owner or the work is exciting to me. Lots of senior executives think like me.

There's a new model for senior execs out there that is very interesting (since I'm there). It's called hire a senior exec at a reduced rate because he can afford to take less since he's already on a couple of pensions. If you haven't guessed, retirement has gone out the window and guys want to keep working. Some companies think them too 'over qualified' – ouch! Those are the guys to look for in a hurry.

Interns sort of go against my natural tendency to hire the best but I was in a position last month where I needed an interpreter full time to work with a foreign client. At $60 an hour that wasn't going to work. A free, experience-seeking intern solved the problem of helping me immensely while giving the young college person incredible experience and insight into my business. Remember that when you hire someone or have them intern for free, make sure they understand the level of complexity, seriousness, etc. of the job you need done. A receptionist you find cheaply can be your worst enemy since that person is the first contact between you and your customer. Think strategically when hiring and please don't take advantage of interns.

Since most people don't need full blown offices consider hiring people who can work for you from their home. Now isn't that a can of worms? A good interview and probation can tell you if that decision was right or wrong.

Considering hiring someone for your dream team can be fraught with twists and turns. There are gems out there for sure. Consider having a second person in the interview to get a different opinion.

Just remember bringing on people effect your business and their life. Don't hire for silly reasons but focus on your task to find the most competent person for the task at hand and you may end up with your own Dream Team.

Networking

Common Principles

Networking is an art form and an exciting way to gather revenue generating connections but a skill that few seem to be able to master

Make sure you know your goals in terms of networking before going to a special gathering or group. Are you making contacts for you or someone else? Do you want to learn something about those businesses you're meeting? Are you sourcing for products or services? The Vancouver Board of Trade is a great place to network but one must be aware the business members there are generally mature, large corporations.

The Burnaby Board of Trade (in a Vancouver suburb) tends to be comprised of more community-based businesses perhaps more sympathetic and more attuned to smaller business. Ask yourself what your goals are in participating in networking meetings so that you will pick groups that will help you get what you are looking for. Some meetings are based more on learning, making contacts and/or volunteering rather than on strictly making business connections.

I asked a client what networking meant to him. He thought pensively and told me 'meeting someone, giving them a business card followed by the elevator pitch and asking them for the sale'. Phew, I almost fell over from the intense meeting which must have occurred and the pure sense of being pounced which the person on the end of that barrage might feel at the moment of impact. That's far from my idea of networking.

I feel networking should be from a position of being a genuine and passionate person interested in helping the other person in the networking equation. Passion and commitment are powerful feelings to convey to another person. It develops a better bond than "hey, you wanna buy a car?"

With the above ambush networking scene in your mind, imagine mine. I meet someone and we exchange pleasantries getting to know each other a little better. I find out what motivates the other guy and think about whether I can utilize his service or buy his product. That's not my first purpose though. I think of all the people I know and whether there is a real match between this person in front of me and the others I know.

It often ends up that I take two cards because I know someone who is looking for the services of that person. I ask them to call my office for the person's phone number or when I get to my office I'll drop a short note to the client who could use the service.

Nine times out of ten if I make a successful connection, a link up for two people, it will come back to benefit me one day. Karma!

Darcy Rezac, the former Executive Director of the Vancouver Board of Trade, wrote a book on networking and regularly holds seminars to members on how to do effective networking. There's a friendly rivalry between Darcy and Peter Newman as to who invented networking. Again there is a psychology to networking or shall we call it common sense?

When you go to a networking event print your first name larger on those proffered name tags we hate and put it on your right lapel. Why, because people prefer to look there rather your chest especially if you are woman. Also, if they should know you but can't remember your name it is easier to read with their peripheral vision - gee how simple.

In a two hour stand-up networking meeting one should be able to leave the event with 18-20 business cards. Fewer and you've spent too much time chatting and not enough networking. Now if you have no agenda, talk to one or two people but bear in mind you will probably mess up their agenda of 18 business cards or their purpose for networking. You have to define your purpose prior to the networking as one where you will be an interested schmoozer or a hunter.

I always go to the high powered networking events with a colleague of mine, a 'partner or wing man'. My partner for the evening is also my safety valve. In the terrible event I run into someone who is very bad at networking and wants to talk about the colliding of neutrons in the space time continuum in relation to the black hole theory, I have an out! I may know more about that than he does but would hate to bore someone with the theoretical constructs,

Yes, I have an out. If my colleague is paying attention I will make the small re-arranged signal like raising my hand to my right ear signifying; help me quickly the guy can't network, is boring me and get me outta here. My colleague will then come over to the pair of us and politely break into the conversation saying he has someone across the floor that is dying to meet me.

My theory is if you have no interpersonal skills then you shouldn't try to network with a master and stay home.

After an evening of networking I will go home and make quick notes on the back of business cards I've gathered. The notes could be reminders of who I should pass the card onto or perhaps I've promised the card owner a flyer or an email. I must admit I've put 'avoid at all costs' on the back of more than a couple of cards. I then use my business card and scan all my new contacts into my Maximizer database management system for later.

Sometimes I'll send a quick email to the person I enjoyed the night before thanking them for the chat. The guys who sell insurance and try to do a sales pitch on me before I even get into the office on my blackberry that night get evicted from my database. *Hey, I'm Canadian, we are polite and don't like pushy.*

Successful Business Networking

Effective business networking is the linking together of individuals who, through relationship building, become walking, talking advertisements for one another. If you don't have anything in common with the person you are talking to you may know someone in your circle who does.

The best networking happens when you meet another entrepreneur and think is there anyone I know to whom I can introduce this person? I think it's the karma principal. Don't have any preconceptions about trying to sell anything to this person but how you can help them using your connections. It will come back to you in spades. Keep in mind that networking is about being genuine and authentic, building trust and relationships, and seeing how you can help others.

Make sure you know your goals in terms of networking before going to a special group. Are you making contacts for you or someone else? Do you want to learn something about those businesses you're meeting? Some meetings are based more on learning, making contacts, and/or volunteering rather than on strictly making business connections.

Visit a number of networking groups to see which ones spark your interest in terms of focus, interest, support, and relevance to what you are trying to accomplish. Is your industry represented already? Notice the tone and attitude of the group. Do the people sound supportive of one another? Does the leadership appear competent? Many groups will allow you to visit a few times before joining. Meetup.com is a great place to find networking opportunities in your geographic area and are free to join.

The best networking happens when you join a special interest group, association or group that you can volunteer in. By giving your expertise, offering a role in management or working to a common purpose you will gain more knowledge of the inner workings of the group, become more visible to others and may even be considered an expert in the field. I joined an import/export association, became a director and learned an awful lot about running a trading business.

Because I'm a Director of the import/export association people consider me an expert but I have a lot to learn. This is also a great way to give back to groups that have helped you.

The more visible you become in your volunteer positions, social networking sites the more people will see you as the expert in your field and will come to you for advice. Become known as a powerful resource for others. When you are known as a strong resource, people remember to turn to you for suggestions, ideas, names of other people, etc. This keeps you visible to them.

You must identify your own Unique Selling Proposition. What I mean is – what differentiates you from others in your industry and why would someone use you and your services over others? In order to get referrals at a networking event, you must first have a clear understanding of what you do that you can easily articulate to others.

Listen! Be aware of what you are looking for and how others can help you in your business. Listen for the opportunity to make yourself a hero to a colleague or friend who owns a business and to the person you are meeting. I've made relationships with undying gratitude because I have hooked up people that made business dealings who would never have met otherwise.

I'll say this again. The best networking results from you thinking about the person in front of you and how you can help them and someone in your network as well.

Chapter Ten

Finding the Entrepreneur Within

Develop Your Confidence

I have a client who is a petrochemical consultant and she charges enormous amounts of money. After much soul searching and support from my team she decided to charge $200/hour which was a mid level price for her services.

She worked for 3 months for her big oil company client. I asked her how her accounts receivable were coming along and she sheepishly admitted she hadn't billed them a nickel yet. What? She explained that she was afraid that her bill was too high.

After peeling myself off the floor I realized this is too common, people doubting their worth, their quality and the lack of confidence to even send a bill for services rendered.

Doubt Kills the Warrior

You're a new **Entrepreneur** and you have gone to school, or not; have a business plan, or not: have money for your venture, or not. However, you have initiated your start-up.

You can have all your marketing research, business skills under your belt, money for your startup, maybe even a partner who provides synergy to your skills and talents. But there's a problem. It's nagging, stronger than anything you've ever experienced in your old employment scenario and it is, unfortunately, debilitating. **It is DOUBT!**

So you get a meeting with the big boss for your pitch and the meeting goes really well. He is impressed with your company and **now he wants a QUOTE – yikes!!**

For years when I was a commercial photographer I had the fear that my quote was too high, not high enough, that I wasn't good enough to play this game and so on. Having doubt in your early business development is normal but one must get past the inactivity it creates. It would make me sit on a quote out of fear (doubt) for several days sometimes to the point of losing the contract (and we are talking about many thousands of dollars) all because I was afraid to ask for the money.

The Solution?

Get a <u>Mentor</u> or a Business Coach.

Find a <u>Salesman</u> to make the sales calls.

Find someone to <u>manage</u> your business while you do the aspect of it that you fell in love with in the first place.

<u>Respond in a way you are more comfortable with</u>, email, face to face, or telephone.

Remember, if he asks you for a quote he needs you as much as you need his business.

Success Fuels the Warrior

So now you know how doubt and lack of confidence can be a debilitating aspect of your business success.

I ask new entrepreneur clients to speak to three other entrepreneurs and ask them a series of questions. What was your biggest problem in the first year (usually answered with faulty planning, lack of finance, or planning)?

I also get them to ask the experienced entrepreneur: when did he or she feel they were over the hump with their business?

Speaking of which, some people never seem to get over the hump in their mind. There's always another problem to surmount. When do I make my first big sale? When should I hire my first employee?

For my money, the best ways to feel like you are 'over the hump' is to execute your first big sale, chalk up your first budget breaking sales month or receive kudos from a satisfied client.

Remember – SUCCESS Fuels the Warrior!

As a young photographer, I struggled with charging my clients at the same rate as my peers in the profession. For years I undercut others and secured the business. However, in a moment of bravado I submitted a proposal to a huge political figure to manage the advertising for his campaign. He accepted my bid. My future in commercial photography was assured. The success of that moment, in time, gave me the impetus to continue at a level I had dreamed about in the past. When the doubt is replaced by the feeling of success – watch out world!

An entrepreneur needs to have that moment in time when he feels that he has achieved success. Take it from me, when you grasp that first milestone of success with both hands you will rid yourself of the nagging doubt that likes to creep into our minds and keep you from succeeding in your goals.

Achievement

Business and sports, what do they have in common?

Business is all about money and companies, employees and responsibility, guys in suits and professionals in the form of accountants and lawyers. It's about deadlines and customer service, challenges and obligations. We're not talking the business that marches along doing what is necessary to make money but not exceeding the norm. I'm talking about the corporations you see in the news (in a good light), community involved and one of those businesses that are listed in the Best Places to Work lists.

Vancouver was home to the Olympic Games of 2010 and there was winners and losers – but was there?

I was watching the Snowboard Cross competition, not even an Olympic sport until recently. The guys waiting for the starting gun looked like the boys next door with their unkempt hair tucked under their toques. When I was a skier, we looked on these guys like crazies. As they waited for the gun in their blue jean style bottoms they looked like they were waiting for a beer instead of making a run for a Gold medal in the Olympics. By the way, one of the four young men, Alex

Bilodeau, was the first Canadian to earn a Gold medal on Canadian soil – ever.

Yet there was a comparison to be made between the two, business and sports.

The Olympics are about Achievement.

Allusive to most, for sure, but the fact those Snowboarders got to the Olympics is an achievement that needs, no, demands recognition. In the entire world four young men raced to the bottom of a hill fighting for the Gold medal. I am awestruck to be reminded that these young men worked for four years between Olympics to try for the Gold again. Four years of training, international competitions, fear, doubt, hurt and emotions for a minute of intense action.

The best businesses are successful because, like our four young men, have achieved a high standard of excellence reserved for the elite.

Sports and Business elite, they have everything in common!

Ask for Help

You cannot run the company in a vacuum. Don't be too proud to ask for help. I've sat on my butt trying to fix a problem with an old website for several weeks, heck months before my wife looked at me and said, "Biz, hire someone for crying out loud before you go crazy". Gee, I never thought of that. Well, I did think about it but the cheap side of me said that I could save money by doing it myself. What's that saying about representing yourself in court? You have an idiot for a client.

Let's assume I work on my website struggling with a problem that a pro can fix in a couple of hours. I charge $200 per hour as a professional mentor so I'm spending a small fortune doing it myself when I could be making that money. I can hire a competent web person for $60 an hour to do it right in less time.

I'm reminded of a friend who had a business card that essentially said he did <u>everything</u> including fixing the kitchen sink.

The card said "wars fought, lions tamed, rebellions started, companies run", etc.

Some time later I set up my own business card which really looked very silly after I laid it out because it read like my friend's; corporations setup & managed, marketing campaigns developed & run, employees vetted, financing secured, IPO's started, coaching attempted, consulting, confidence built, workshops created, problems identified, management corrected, companies franchised, locations found, etc.

I think the wonders of a business startup require a jack of all trades. I've been lucky to have worked with over 1000+ of them so far and am constantly amazed at the variety of businesses and problems encountered and the solutions we've been able to find.

That is not to say I can do all of those things. You see, I have professionals behind me who are experts and they have worked with me for many years. Instead of doing all this yourself and/or hiring many professionals look into a mentor.

Everyone needs a mentor, coach, counselor, consultant, or whatever you call him. Take his or her advice. Question it but don't be headstrong and forge ahead on your own. The muddy waters of entrepreneurship are not only cloudy but fraught with hidden shoals, sandbars and whatever other metaphors you can come up with for the dangers facing business today.

At the start of a new business or seeking a handle on the old one, I hope you take the time to work with a professional to setup up some business (and personal) goals for the next year, take your business the next step or maybe give you direction if you are starting up a new venture.

I used to think that coaches and consultants were a drain on my resources rather than the asset they really are to a growing business.

What do you do when the business you started last year is suddenly falling behind in revenues, the economy sucks and you don't know what to do? Your buddy has a similar yet different problem keeping him awake at night. He has fulfillment issues and can't fill orders fast enough creating backlogs, unhappy customers and more. Both have problems – where do you go for help?

A Business Coach will <u>treat you as an equal</u> and collaboratively work out tactics and scenarios for you to work on to take some strain off you and get your business back on track. A Business Consultant will come in as the white knight with solutions to your problems as long as you take his sage advice. You'll pay him the big bucks because you are putting your life and that of your business in his hands. You desperately need him to <u>make decisions for you</u>.

Then there's the Business Counselor (which I am fully certified through APEC and Acadia University). The Counselor uses his practical business experience in the same way as the others noted above but rather than tell you what to do or provide strongly recommended advice to you, he will provide you with insight into the problems facing your business.

By pointing out things relevant to your business that you may or may not be able to do something about, <u>it will be your decision</u>. No recriminations here folks because you may be in trouble but you are calling the shots.

What works best for you is the type of interaction you really need. Some people need the hand holding, others need qualified advice like "what would you do in my situation"; others really can make the decision but don't know all the options available to them.

The **Coach** works with you, the **Consultant** does it for you and the **Counselor** helps you make the choice.

Mentors

Mentors can be a delight. In the early '90's I had reached a point in my photography business where I had to go big or go home and had some issues to deal with including confidence and sales techniques. I took a workshop series on entrepreneurship presented by my now good friend, Carl de Jong, who was with the Business Development Bank at the time. I learned a lot.

One of the good things that came out of it, was I was mentored by a retired photographer who had no agenda other than to help someone in the same field. I wasn't his competition. Photographers are notorious for being aggressively competitive so there is little chance to compare notes with working professionals.

When you are looking for a mentor some traits are obvious like good listening skills, certainly expertise and maturity, wise beyond their years (or just older like me).

I wish more people would use a mentor; it would make life easier for many. A mentor can give you the encouragement to take a leap of faith knowing that the risk is mitigated because the mentor has given you support. Consider a mentor a sounding board to throw those crazy things rattling in your head that you dare not speak, because you thought they might sound crazy. A mentor won't be judgmental just supportive.

I must say that there are also two types of mentors; mentors who can afford to offer advice because they are retired and want to give back to their field and/or others. I am involved with a youth loans fund (Canadian Youth Business Foundation) that has 'volunteer' mentors who are not allowed to spend more than 2 hours per month with their mentees. Obviously this is designed to allow both to focus on specific issues yet also setup so the mentor isn't overwhelmed or used.

The second mentor is the skilled professional who is paid to provide exceptional advice, put forth scenarios, help with presentations and support the mentee at every crossroad. I fit into the latter paid mentoring.

Mentoring Others

You can network and learn a lot by mentoring others. Mentoring can take place on a couple of levels; firstly, a photographer mentoring another photographer may be in my situation; older passing on the reins to a younger generation. The second mentor is one who is a specialist in an aspect of the business and mentors a business to help that one specific area. I had a volunteer mentor who worked with one of my clients on her financials for an entire day for free.

Paying It Forward, Serving humanity, Giving Back, Adding Value to others – what the heck is going on?

Tony Robbins espouses serving humanity as the next step to personal greatness, Oprah talks about paying it forward as the step to personal fulfillment, Michael Gerber told me the next great entrepreneurial model has a component to his business that gives back to the community as part of a grand plan.

What the heck is going on? The business world is changing. I see young people volunteering to help the homeless, I see people becoming mentors to struggling entrepreneurs, people giving of themselves to be role models to others and people finding a mission bigger than themselves. The entire world is changing.

As Tony Robbins says "a meaningful life is about 'we' not me". What a great society if that were true.

What kind of world would we have if we defined a new level of business success? If we:

Paid our success forward to others.

Added more value to our lives by helping others.

Found a purpose in helping others attain what we have.

Could be a role model to people who needed us.

Realized that there are a lot of people worse off than us.

I use a hybrid technique of coaching, mentoring, counseling and consulting. They are so distinct that I typically use a bit of each. Some clients want advice (mentoring) some want immediate results so I tell them what to do (Consulting), some want to be guided to their end decision (Coaching) and some want to be guided but in the end decide themselves (Counseling).

When I was looking to change careers, I was always alone in my search; I never considered that a mentor in the field could save me endless pain in searching, making the wrong turns and starting a career at the wrong junction so to speak. Imagine a college grad starting in the mail room (classic example, sorry) of a large corporation and thinking they would move up the ladder to become CEO by starting at the ground level. A mentor might suggest methods to go into the marketing department as an intern or a similar role that would give better results faster. The more experience we have, of course, the more people we know so there is the possibility that mentors can fast track a client.

Most people want to be told what to do to get from point A to point B. Most people also want to be validated. I often point this out to them and ask them if they want me just to agree with them or do they want valuable advice. This is critical because people don't really know what they need; they know what they want but rarely the former. I will not tell people what they want to hear. I have a client who wanted to buy three radio stations out of the country and kept me on the phone for an hour talking about the value of the opportunity.

Even with me telling him it was a ludicrous idea, he continued until I suddenly realized he wanted me to agree with him. I confronted him and he said, yes, he wanted my approval. I asked him if he could afford to lose the millions and he said he could, so I told him to go ahead. He did and lost all his investment money within months. He sheepishly apologized for doubting my 'wisdom' the next time we met. I raised my hourly fee after that.

There are several sources for mentors. There are sites online allowing people to get free mentoring, Mentor Hub on LinkedIn, a family friend in the industry you want to break into and finally a retired person from that same industry. With BizzoBoard.com we are providing a free mentoring service with simple problems which if addressed in minutes can be free to the mentee.

However, in most cases, that simple question becomes a problem of Goliath proportions requiring considerable effort from a mentor. This is a paid situation. In a career situation, having a mentor read a resume and offer advice is fine but what if that mentor is being asked to read resumes, covering letters for each job, rewrites, coaching etc.; endless hours comes to mind.

The unfortunate aspect of calling yourself a mentor is that people assume it is free. I judicially use mentoring both ways, providing free support and answers to questions that are simple. If the situation is more complex I charge a fee.

I struggled for years in my first business as a commercial photographer so I understand the need for a mentor. It took me ten years to be able to ask the price I knew I was worth in the beginning. Had I searched for a mentor, I would have zoomed forward in my career instead of growth at a snails pace, exerting energies in all the wrong places. I am a mentor so I can save people that angst. I also love working with creative people in setting up a business for the first time.

The best mentoring relationship will give the mentee advice based on years of experience. Whether it's volunteer or fee-based advice, it is worth the time spent to foster the relationship.

Chapter Eleven
New Methods or Ways to Do Business

Success in your business may come naturally but most likely it will take a lot of effort and may come from doing your business in a different manner than most.

Innovation is the result of the mother of invention. If you can't conduct business in the usual manner make people follow your new method. Social media, blogging, and the Internet in general reflect the new frontier of methods to find, secure or keep customers.

A client who owns a 'Zen' garage in Vancouver found his new way of doing business in the '90's. His family had run a garage in the same location for three generations. With the Internet came opportunity for my client. With a new generation running the show they decided to go with the innovations created by the Internet.

They bought specialized software that allowed them to have computers at the bay where each mechanic worked so they could order parts from inventory and bill the client as they worked. They built a website allowing them to be able to book appointments for customers online. The next step was giving each mechanic wireless headsets so when a customer called to check on their vehicle they were patched through to the mechanic as he worked on their car. This innovation not only increased their customer base but increased productivity and sales. They were also the first website I know of who targeted hyper-local customers. These were implemented in 1995 way ahead of its time.

Eight Tips for the Budding Entrepreneur

It's Great Being Small – I like to keep my businesses small and close to my chest. It doesn't mean I do the work, it means, as a rule, I contract people to do it for me. Being small allows you to make decisions quickly and move faster than the big guys. Have a product that is not selling? Dump it – being small allows you to do that. Imagine the other big guys making the same decisions that take weeks because they have 'decision by committee'. They must do a study, an analysis then a report before making a decision, ahggh.

Don't Be Afraid – You've already taken the first big step; you've decided to start your own business. What's the worse that can happen? You could lose your shirt perhaps. But hey, been there done that a few times. Fear leads me to my number three tip.

Failure Breeds Experience which Creates Success – As Zig Ziglar once said, "If you learn from defeat, you haven't really lost." I've given so many speeches about starting your own business, I must tell you that the response I get when I tell people about my failures creates more buzz than you can imagine. I've raised hundreds of thousands of dollars in days for a business and closed the doors a year later without selling a thing. Is that a record? LOL, no, but it goes to show that failure gives you more tools with which to work. It's called "what not to do the next time." I celebrate these 'ah ha' moments. If you fall down a couple of times and learn from it you will be successful. I'm not saying you need to lose your first or second businesses, consider that maybe you've made a couple of mistakes on your new business and you learn from it. That's the point.

Act on Your Impulse – If you think that new product you've added to your line is incredible, tell the world, maybe your instincts are correct. Don't be afraid to get it out there. Equally important, don't hesitate to stop an action you've begun that isn't going anywhere.

Procrastination – I knew an entrepreneur who spent months doing market research on a new product. Eventually, after incredible research proved a demand for the product, he quit his business and went back to school. The problem – he wasn't an entrepreneur. He delayed his business opening by doing impeccable, albeit over-kill, research – it's called avoidance. He was afraid to actually do the business. This would be the time to decide if you really are an entrepreneur.

Guerrilla Marketing – Five short years ago it took considerable money to launch a business in the form of brochures, business cards, complex websites and so on. Today Social Media Networking allows for a blog to be made for a few hundred dollars that you can easily manage on your own, QR codes instead of brochures and Social media sites that get you around the world in seconds. Utilize them; abuse them, that is the fun of being a guerrilla.

Coffee Buddies – Stay away from those who think they are entrepreneurs but live precariously day to day from gleaning energy and ideas from you. A one hour coffee meeting shooting the breeze costs me hundreds of dollars so it's important for me to prioritize my time. People need people, don't get me wrong, but understand some people want your ideas and some just want coffee. They have nothing to do and nothing is going on in their business. Given a choice, I'd rather have an enjoyable coffee with friends.

What's Your Focus? – A former client told me the other day that his moving business has gone crazy in the three years since he started. He told me he doubled his revenue in the second year then decided to hire someone to take away the things in his business he hated doing like accounting, sales calls, and collection. With the new hire in place for one year, he doubled the company revenues again. Great thinking!

The Healer vs. the Corporate Wellness Coach

I had an interesting client years ago who came in asking for help starting her business. Let me describe her first. She was in her early 50's, rubenesque, wearing a caftan with her hair pulled back in a ponytail framing a cherubic face.

When I asked her about her business idea she calmly told me in a low voice – I am a healer. I felt like saying Namaste at that point but asked her further questions. Now please remember in 2002 a healer was someone below a soothsayer in terms of business careers.

Going forward I asked her more and it became clear she was a well educated woman dedicated to helping people and one to be taken seriously. I asked her how she earned money for her healing and she said each hour was billed at between $10 - 60 per hour. I asked her how she differentiated the price and she told me that someone like me would obviously pay $60 and someone without means would pay $10/hour. The obvious question I posed to her was "are both hours the same?" She agreed that, obviously, an hour was an hour.

I suggested to her that we change her focus and charge everyone $60 per hour until she reached a certain monthly earning goal at which time she would offer one Friday a month free sessions to those who can't afford it. She liked the idea! I knew then I had to work with her.

After 10 weeks of intensive business plan development I asked her to present her plan to a group of my advisors in a boardroom. She strode into the boardroom in a business suit with a briefcase, a confidence never before seen and an attitude that spoke authority.

She introduced herself, "Hi I'm _____. I am a Corporate Wellness Coach specializing in medium to large corporations. I charge $60 and hour". She then proceeded to outline her 'business' of helping people in a structured wellness-based manner. She had made an unbelievable transformation. Part of me felt like I had created a monster while part of me was happy she had found a way to reach more people.

She did have a successful business and yes she reached a happy medium between the gentle healer and the corporate coach.

How to Keep Yourself Happy in Your Own Business

Much has been spoken about how to make money, how to find customers, how to make conversions on marketing material or how to manage your business effectively. Does anyone actually advise small business owners on how to deal with the running of a business at a personal level?

I see people making milestones of business success in terms of money. I'm wondering if we can itemize some aspects of our business life that business people can be happy while doing what they love to do.

Practice time management

If you work 10 hours a day because you can never 'find the time' to do a consistently adequate job of operating your company, set up a system of time management and/or hire more people to help

How much money do you really need to earn?

Is pure materialism the absolute goal for your business life or can you live a more meaningful and fulfilled life by slowing down that driving urge to have all the toys? In my life, I am totally enjoying having time for myself without having tons of employees, a huge office and people demanding my time. I can allocate time to those things I enjoy and still make the same money.

Love what you do

Every business I ever started was through a lifestyle choice, something I loved or was passionate about, otherwise, why do it. I tell my wife I have a business vocation (management consulting) and I have an avocation (my social media). I guess I have convinced myself somewhere along the way that instead of working 20 hours a day I'd work 4-6 hours a day at my business and a few hours having fun at my 'hobby' – social media. Hey, if you have to trick your brain so be it!

Keep the people in your life who are important to keep you happy

Ha, does that even need to be said? Of course; how many businesses were made in the ruination of families and relationships? Don't allow yourself to be controlled by those emotions which will take you out, alienate your family, lose your closest friends and cause you to end up divorced. Ask any wealthy person who made their fortunes that way and they will have regrets.

Be Honorable

Duh, well who starts out to be a sneaky conniving fraudster? The answer is that no one does, but if you run your business ethically, have an abiding concern for your clients/customers and run your business with honor and respect others will see it, people will come to you and your business will thrive. The thing I dream about when doing business is to be honorable in my dealings. If you're an ass you will attract bad karma and bad business. You may make some quick money but you won't last in business. You mess with me once and that's the last time you will. The old adage, the golden rule, is so appropriate in business, treat your customers and suppliers and even your competition with respect and honor.

Keep learning while you run your company

From experience I can tell you that if you are in a state of constantly finding answers, learning all that there is to know about your business and searching for new alternatives to old problems you will never burn out. I find education fun and have spent over 15 years in post secondary education – I have a need to learn and it keeps my game sharp.

Take care of your health

If you lose your health running your business you have nothing. Guys who constantly move the 'cocktail hour' closer to noon than after work, the guys who eat fast food to 'save time' and don't exercise because they don't have the discipline are creating a problem that will blow up in their faces.

All I'm saying is run your business like it is your child, face problems immediately, take care of relationships and make sure you are going to be around to see your kids go to college.

Chapter Twelve
Some Other Considerations

The Business Startup

I specialize in helping people setup new businesses. When you mention startups people often think of the old dot com model where millions of bucks were at stake. Wikipedia says, *"A startup company or startup is a company with a limited operating history. These companies, generally newly created, are in a phase of development and research for markets. The term became popular internationally during the dot-com bubble when a great number of dot-com companies were founded"*

I work with newly created businesses usually under $500k in funds. The startups I work with are started from dreams, money that's been saved (unlike the dot-coms approach to OPM- other people's money), lack a plan and think on their feet.

Some observations I've had about setting up new enterprises:

Think big but also have milestones so you will get some satisfaction by reaching them. There's nothing more disillusioning to think a million dollars is in your reach in the first year when in fact it'll be more like $50k after the startup process and implementation phase. Most people fail to get sustainable in the first year.

The big guys think about running lean and talk about burn rates. Forget the burn rate; you don't even need to know what that means. Remember you will need your money for operating capital so be lean. Buy used equipment, make deals and don't feel like you are a millionaire until you have it in your pocket. I have a client who had a great profit at the end of year one and spent the entire bundle on a new fleet of trucks, yikes! Not the thing to do. This would have been a good operating line for the beginning of year two.

My friend, Michael Gerber, tells entrepreneurs to have a robust system from the start and pretend it is for future expansion; so think big here. It takes a lot of work but can be as simple as a

Procedures Manual. Wikipedia identifies a process similar called Iteration –"Iteration means the act of repeating a process usually with the aim of approaching a desired goal or target or result. Each repetition of the process is also called iteration, and the results of iteration are used as the starting point for the next iteration."

Spend an inordinate amount of time researching and developing your market and how you will get there. Gone are the days when you opened a store and people just came to shop. Maybe that would work if you were a general store in the old west but not today, sorry.

If you ask an entrepreneur how much time he works on his business each week the response may seem ludicrous. I estimate a busy entrepreneur will easily spend 80 hours a week trying to make the business work. Being an entrepreneur is not for the faint of heart. What's my point? Not to scare you off because all the work you do, will be for you. I'm suggesting you need a good balance between work and a life. How many marriages have blown up because of this? You started your business so you can have control, so make sure you take time for yourself, maybe a golf game in the middle of the week or an early dinner with your wife. BTW lose the BlackBerry for the evening.

Women Make Better Entrepreneurs!

Guys – Please close your eyes for a moment or skip this section because you won't like this one at all!

Women make better Businessmen – oops- entrepreneurs!

Some interesting stats from the Women's Enterprise Center in Vancouver (2009):

Women own and operate **35 per cent** of small businesses in B.C. or almost **137,000 businesses**, which is higher than the national average of just under 34%.

The number is expected to **double** over the next decade. In ten years, it is estimated that **264,000 B.C. women** will own and operate businesses.

There are more than **821,000 women entrepreneurs in Canada.**

Women in Canada make up a larger share of the self-employed than in any other country.

Women contribute in excess of **$18 billion** to the Canadian economy each year.

Since 1976, the average annual **growth rate for self-employed women** has been **5.3%** compared with 2.2% for men.

One-third of self employed Canadians are women.

Women entrepreneurs hold ownership in about **45% of Canadian small and medium enterprises**.

The likelihood of self-employment with women **increases with age and most women are aged 35 to 54**.

The age of those who start a business is gradually increasing (**currently 33% of startups are over the age of 45**).

The most rapid growth is among women **around 55 years**.

So what? These figures don't prove that women are better entrepreneurs, but there are definite trends giving me pause to believe the even though they own less businesses they turn out more successful ones. My research, which is based on hands-on knowledge of over 1000 startups, indicates that most of the successfully run enterprises are owned by women. There could be a number of reasons:

Are women better organized?
Maybe women are better as team builders focusing on working with others rather than be the lone wolf?
Perhaps women are more financially prudent and good at bootstrapping?
Are women better networkers? Some of my twitter followers believe so.
Women generally aren't the risk taking, which men are so good at, maybe better planning by women results in better choices and success?

Bloomberg BusinessWeek said, "**Women business owners are frequently cited as one of the fastest growing segments in entrepreneurship**". Why do you think that may be true?

Women ask for help, have different values than men, and may be less prone to taking risk. Women are more educated than in the past, and based on business success as employees, have more confidence too when they open their own business.

According to the Center for Women's Business Research, between 1997 and 2004, privately held, woman-owned businesses grew at three times the rate of all U.S. privately held firms, and woman-owned businesses created jobs at twice the rate of all other firms. Furthermore, women did all of this with less than 1% of the venture capital that's invested in small businesses.

Women tend to be value driven, men go for the bucks – not to create sexist stereotypes about men and women, here folks – men love machinery, and women give birth. I know a lot of male entrepreneurs who are value-driven and female ones who are money-driven, suggesting there aren't great differences.

CNN reminded me the other day (Mother's Day) about the top women, in this case also mothers, who shaped the world with their successful businesses.

Gerber – Dorothy Gerber figured there had to be a better way to make baby food and her husband agreed. Most of you have been nurtured by her decision.

Mrs. Fields – A 20 year old woman developed a cookie business for mass production and is now in thousands of malls in the US.

Savvymom.ca – Was conceived over a Starbucks non-fat latte in December 2004, when two former university roommates, Sarah and Minnow, met and decided mom's needed practical solutions to be stay at home moms.

Mary Kay Ash – Said "You can't keep determined people from success". What can you say about a woman who took a good product and created entrepreneurs from countless other women? She made women completely independent for the first time in their lives.

Estee Lauder- Famous cosmetologist said "If you don't sell, it's not the product that's wrong – it's you".

Oprah Winfrey – What can you say about the billionaire media mogul? Wow.

Ariana Huffington – She is perhaps one of the most successful female Internet entrepreneurs and is the founder of the top blog in the world according to Technorati!

Baby Einstein – When mom Julie Aigner-Clark went looking for educational materials for her newborn daughter in 1996, she couldn't find educational items that helped her child so she started a highly successful business.

When everything is said and done, given equal opportunities, women will rise to any man's achievement. I've known and worked with so many more women entrepreneurs it always begs the question – Are they better?

Sources:

Prime Minister's Task Force on Women Entrepreneurs, Nov. 2003

BC Stats Small Business Profile, 2003

CIBC's Look at New Entrepreneurs in Canada, June 2004

HRDC Survey of Self Employment in Canada

A Portrait of Small Business Growth and Employment in Western Canada – Western Economic Diversification

The Reluctant Entrepreneur

I was asked to consult with 'Clive', a British immigrant entrepreneur who owned a company back east, who needed some help with raising operating capital. Now, this can be an easy 'show me the money' scenario based on sound management, a great business plan and a wonderful innovative product or it can become a finger pointing analytical dissection of a business in turmoil. Clive unfortunately is the latter.

Most management consultants will tell you the three most important parts of a successful corporation are good management, enough capital and a great product. The theory is if you have two of the three you can ALWAYS find the third. I agree with this because time and time again this scenario is played out in boardrooms all over North America.

My client told me his friend Clive needed $3M to get his troubled company back 'on track' so that a consortium could utilize his revolutionary prototype to fill a huge multinational contract. *Sounds good I think!* Hmmm. Something is wrong here. I call the entrepreneur and have a conference call during which he tells me he needs $5M (it started out at $3M the day before). I bluntly asked him about the difference and he said some of his staff had not been paid in a year and he felt they should get something. *Bad vibes now flowing.*

I suggest people who might be able to help him out and then the exceptions start coming out. I tell him my angel investors will need control of the corporation; *No way he says*; "I've put my blood and guts into the business". I tell him the very least we'll need is to replace the CFO (Chief Financial Officer) with our own guy to oversee expenditures. *No way* the entrepreneur proclaimed, "The current CFO is my buddy!" My next comment infuriates the entrepreneur when I coldly tell him most of his management team needs to be replaced with qualified people, *but they're my friends* he tells me. I ask him in his role as CEO, what is his background. He's an engineer and academic. Therein lays the answer to my growing concerns. This is another entrepreneurial dream lacking direction and substance while being run by an academic. Here's an inventor and a nice guy who is a reluctant entrepreneur and CEO.

I thought of numerous solutions to his problem in the days after I spoke with him and the more I thought about it the more incensed I became. Clive had broken all the rules:

hired his friends because he was comfortable with them,

he had undercapitalized the corporation thereby running out of cash when it was needed,

was afraid to give up control (what's 100% of nothing?),

wanted to create a legacy for his employees without taking care of them, had an arrogance born of ignorance,

was afraid to manage except by consensus,

felt everyone was out to get him,

didn't understand the concept of shareholders,

And on and on...

Good management requires tough decisions. If you have built a business on a house of cards it will fall down and nothing except a major overhaul will fix the problem. When Clive arbitrarily changed the amount he needed from $3 to $5 million dollars he forgot that the investors had earned every cent of their money and his cavalier attitude was infuriating.

The sad effect of all this discussion is that a lot of people who can't afford it will lose a lot of money and an incredible revolutionary product will be lost to the world because of mismanagement.

Being an entrepreneur is not for the faint of heart and perhaps some people should stay academics.

Franchise Businesses

For some a franchise is the ideal way for you to get into business. It's typically a good opportunity, well thought out, established and comes with training.

For a Small Medium Enterprise (SME) to enter into a franchise opportunity one must weigh the options of how unique the business is, can it be replicated without buying a franchise and does the 'turnkey' aspect of the franchise make it both affordable and quicker to get into operation.

Control is extremely important to the franchiser as it maintains the brand, provides the franchiser hands on control and provides them a percentage of your business forever. As a franchisee you must sign specific exclusive contracts outlining your obligations to the 'brand', your intention to follow all of the franchiser's regulations and to purchase each and every product or service that you sell from the parent company.

An efficient and well run franchise will generate you a lot of money but a marginal franchise can be fraught with delivery issues, support and lack of support when needed. Even a well run franchise like Tim Horton's will cost you over $600,000 to get in the door and they will say that after paying your salary as the owner/operator you will earn $75k on sales of $1.5M. Franchisers know their stuff to the point that your dream of being an entrepreneur will be dashed by the fact that there are no surprises, no control and longer than average hours of work.

Jurisdictional issues are another obstacle to you and a protection for the franchiser. Imagine buying a t-shirt company in Vancouver, with low sales and little support on the horizon you try to increase sales by opening an eBay store and selling online. Unless the franchiser had been asleep he would have thought of the internet as a sales tool already. By selling online you would be 'trespassing' on someone else's territory just as if you had moved in and opened a store.

Under English common law you would be open to recourse by the franchiser and would need to compensate and probably close it down immediately. Besides that obvious example how does the franchise deal with complex health issues for example in provinces, cities and communities when they are a US based company? Have they taken into consideration labour market trends, socio-economic or cultural concerns?

Territories, exclusivity are the main controls of the franchise company and protect these rights diligently and above all else. Legal options are immediate and remedies are according to the extensive contract you signed. Consider a medium school photography business in a suburb of Vancouver servicing the province of BC. To better serve the clients the photo company franchises several out of the way communities. All is fine until a school on the border calls head office to find a photographer and the HO gives them the name of the neighboring franchise because the territory was loosely defined. Problems need to be addressed and egos are bruised and income is lost. These are complicated issues which need to be addressed and issues that the client has no idea of and wouldn't care anyhow.

Exclusivity can also be further defined by larger territories, e.g. instead of franchising several territories in British Columbia, a national franchiser may give a master license for all of BC and that franchisee can then set up numerous locations. That's not a bad setup if the main corporation is in a distant province.

The bottom line is franchises work for some people and are a bane to the real entrepreneur. The thought that the franchise is safe and secure and will provide good income for some time can be a nurturing consideration for most people. However, in these economic times even Starbucks (which is not a franchise) is closing stores. The recourse for a franchise that goes bankrupt is a big problem and would tie up your business for years.

Rebranding a Company or Product

A company has a good brand, recognized all over the world and sold in the hundreds of millions. Why would they want to change their name, their image or their marketing direction?

Remember when Coke became New Coke? I switched to Pepsi and never went back.

Changing a brand can be a disaster, as Coke found out, when they lost considerable numbers of customers to Pepsi. Changing the name of a product can truly be risky because it creates the illusion of turmoil. There may have been a change of ownership; or maybe the product changed. If you are going to change the name of a product at least make it meaningful to the product.

A company CEO will be the first to tell you that the brand recognition of a company is one of its biggest assets and the basis for the company's reputation. CEO's today are becoming more brand-conscious, as the CEO of FedEx, Frederick W. Smith said: "Maintaining this reputation and its brand image is a top priority for me, since it is one of the most valuable things the company has".

Take some recent changes to the product **Electrosol**; it became **Finish**, a ridiculous name in most marketers' minds with the silly references to diamonds that seems to be geared to the masses without brains. As Electrosol said recently, "FINISH products are the same ELECTRASOL® and JET-DRY® products that you know and trust which are now backed by the power of the world's #1 dishwashing brand."

Stuart Elliott from the New York Times references an email from James Watson, the Marketing Director for Finish, it confirms they are doing the rebranding to consolidate the various names of products into individual global brand entities. A big mistake.

Brinks Home Alarms rebranded itself to **Broadview Home Security**. If you are like me when I see an armored car going down the street I say there goes Brinks whether it is or not. Why would anyone change the name of a household/business classic? Let's change Wells Fargo while we are at it. Broadview Home Security announced on their website that, "Our new name reflects our growth and better represents all we offer our customers, but what we stand for remains the same, building on more than 25 years as Brink's Home Security". Let's come back to Broadway in five years and see if their strategy worked or backfired.

There are several reasons to rebrand an existing product.

The world is getting smaller so a product sold worldwide may want to be consistent and reduce costs.

Maybe the brand is worn out and needs refurbishing, hard to think of one here but maybe Aunt Jemima pancake mix comes to mind.

Mergers happen and good companies get swallowed, how about Canadian Airlines being swallowed by Air Canada.

Maybe the product has suffered a debilitating setback and needs to change the name to find new customers. Remember the Jack-in-the-Box health problems. It's a wonder they recovered. On the other hand Maple Leaf Foods in Canada weathered the storm some years ago by being open and transparent, fixing the problems and gained respect for their brand.

To capitalize on new media, YouTube, Social media and the internet in general.

Just some ideas to make you wonder the next time you see a giant conglomerate make big changes.

Alternative Corporations- An Overview of Social Enterprises, Societies & Charities

I've met many people who want a business in theory but when pressed, really want something else. You probably know that person too. The young idealist inspired by Deepak Chopra to start a yoga studio but feels it should be free or by donation. Looks like a business, acts like a business in some respects, but is it? It is in fact a non-profit based quasi-society wrapped up to look like a business. That is OK.

Not all of us are cut out to be entrepreneurs, business minds or capitalists. Some people are inspired to want to make a change in the world. Run like a business, these organizations are created for change and are run by different rules than a 'normal' business.

Firstly, in Canada, Foundations, Social Enterprises, not-for profit Societies and Charities must be incorporated federally.

A Foundation provides funding to other charities so if you setup a society you can get funding from these organizations and government.

One way to make a Society more than a not for profit, is to start an arms length or create a related Social enterprise corporation. While it doesn't have charitable status it can give receipts to individuals and companies. The receipts would be written off under advertising or promotions.

It takes five directors to start a society in my jurisdiction. It needs bylaws, purpose and a charter. Once it is approved you can apply for charitable status. It takes months to years to get charitable status to be able to issue charitable receipts.

Charity, in the legal sense, describes four areas.

A charitable corporation must be set up to carry out activities in one or all of these areas. They are:

Relief of poverty;

Advancement of education;

Advancement of religion; and

Other purposes beneficial to the community, as determined by the courts, but not falling under any of the above.

It is important that the object clauses clearly describe the activities the corporation will carryout. It is not acceptable simply to reproduce the four principal areas of charity.

Clearly the society you want to setup would be the latter. A charity must benefit the community or a large part of the community – not only a few people. For example, raising funds for one person who suffers from a disease is not considered charitable because it provides a benefit only to that person. Raising funds for disease research is considered charitable because, while only the people who suffer from the disease benefit directly from research, the community as a whole benefits from decreased health care costs and decreased risk of contracting the disease.

The cost of setting all this up is the same as incorporating, $400 if you do it yourself and $1000+ if you have a lawyer in Canada do it.

Grounds for refusing applications for charitable organizations

The following are some of the reasons for which the Public Guardian and Trustee may refuse to approve an application to incorporate a charitable organization:

Objects are not wholly and exclusively charitable

Objects are too broad or are vague

The power clauses include a purpose which is not legally charitable

There are concerns that the proposed charity will not be properly administered, considering a previous failure of the incorporators to comply with the law relating to charities

The organization has been operating as an unincorporated association and its financial documents show that a disproportionate amount of charitable funds are being used for non-charitable purposes or administrative expenses

The name of the organization does not reflect the purposes set out in the application

The organization is primarily promoting private members' interests or benefits

The organization is pursuing political purposes

The organization's liabilities exceed its assets

Some examples of non profit societies:

Paul Brainerd is a former journalist who founded the desktop publishing program PageMaker. He started the Brainerd Foundation, in 1995, which focuses on environmental protection in the Pacific Northwest.

Bill Neukom and Scott Oki (both formerly of Microsoft) created Social Venture Partners. It's a nonprofit philanthropic organization that applies the tactics of venture capitalism to tackling social and environmental issues.

Pierre Omidyar, founder of eBay, chose a similar model. He launched the Omidyar Network in 2004. He called the organization a mission-based investment group, which means they fund for-profits and nonprofits that promote equal access to information, tools and opportunities; connections around shared interests; and a sense of ownership for participants.

Social enterprises are social mission driven organizations which trade in goods or services for a social purpose. Their choice to deliver on financial, social and environmental performance targets is often referred to as having a <u>triple bottom line</u>.

An example of social enterprise includes a Vancouver based restaurant which hires mentally challenged adults to produce their products and serve their customers. Profits are plowed back to the enterprise to use in its operation. Money can also be sent to the foundation overseeing the operation.

Separating Home & Business

I dreamed of being an entrepreneur so I could manage my own life, create my own opportunities, be the man I always wanted to be and be able to work when and where I wanted.

I always wanted to have an office in my house and be independent. As recently, as 1999, businesses were not really considered professional or a serious enterprise unless it was located in a retail or office environment. The huge expense of overhead came with the joys of doing business in the corporate world. My office overhead in downtown Vancouver 13 years ago cost me $15,000 a month just to open the doors.

The advent and change in thinking where working from a 'home office' was long in coming but embraced by all of us.

The problem with working from home has always been focus. The joy of working when you get up in the morning and in your housecoat quickly illustrates the focus issue or lack thereof. I would falter on a regular basis and watch my three favourite TV programs before starting work at eleven.

I would take any opportunity to find alternatives to work. There was the morning newspaper, the dishes that needed to be washed; the neighbor knowing I worked from home would come over for a coffee. He was on employment insurance so it mattered nothing to him that I had to make a living. I welcomed him with open arms anyway. In one instance my coffees with my unemployed buddy moved from coffee, to lunch and then to hours of darts at the local pub – a definite plan for disaster!

It takes effort to create a workspace at home. A client realizing she needed organization made a major change in her family home. She created an office in a third bedroom placed a sign on the door in a light-hearted attempt to show that it's a place of work. She had a business phone line put in and refused to answer calls from her private home phone. She told her friends not to interrupt her between 9-5, stopped doing housework and set aside regular lunch and regular breaks where she would leave the house and walk around the block for 15 minutes.

Some tips:

Establish your own workspace at home that is only used for that purpose.

Make a sign for the office door so if it's closed your family will respect it as an office, keep it light though; your family lives there after all.

Schedule your day and don't mix housecleaning with work.

It's easy to work too much from home funny enough. Know when to stop for the day or your family will start wishing you had a nine to fiver.

Know when you work best and try to master the compromise of it all. I personally work better late at night so my workday tends to reflect that schedule.

Since your overhead is less, consider not taking all the work that comes your way, find people you can refer work to but make sure you get a commission.

Organization will make or break you. I have an unsightly office but as they say "I know where everything is". I have a large 4'x8' digital white board in my office which is my lifesaver.

Chapter Thirteen

You've Made It or Not! Now What?

Making It or Not

Every business I've ever mentored runs in perpetual crisis mode. Think about it. Clients demand better service, ask for things you can't provide, bills come in on time but the invoices are still sitting in the accounts payable basket. There are daily operational items that give the entrepreneur stress because everything in the business is new.

Now that you 'have made it', you need to look at your deficiencies even more closely. Do I have a system in place for this eventuality? Can I provide that huge order that I dreamed about and now have Wal-Mart breathing down my neck asking for the delivery? Procedures manuals need to be in place, systems identified and created or hopefully modified from existing systems.

The planning ahead should be relatively easy for the entrepreneur who has made it 'over the hump"; after all, you have created the ultimate business plan when you decided to open the company, right? Go back to the business plan and see what you had considered for your growth options and how you planned to deal with them. You may gain some insight into your newbie entrepreneurial thinking. Mostly, you will probably scratch your head and think, how could I have been so naive. If you are really clever you will rework that living document and come up with some spectacular assessments and solutions before you're hit with a decimating situation.

Now that you have made it, have you got all the right people in place? Do you have an HR department to manage the benefits, taxes, pensions of your now dedicated employees? You know you can't have 'contractors' on your books forever. The IRS or Canada Revenue Service will catch up one day and you will be in a mess. In Canada, a contractor is really an employee if he earns 50% or more of his income solely from you with you providing him with an office space and a computer.

You've heard of the adage, building a better mousetrap? Look at your product or service regularly once you've made it as an entrepreneur and see if there are improvements you can make. It may be that you need to keep up with new technologies and social convention. I've been noticing coffee delivery systems (formerly called makers) are now mainly one cup servings using plastic portion sizes. What brought about that change? Whatever it looks like, you have to be continually adapting to new market trends.

Do you need to reset your goals now that your business is settled? Maybe that big dream of making lots of money needs to be replaced with 'slow down and smell the roses' on weekends. Cut out those 80 hour weeks. It's funny how stress can change from worrying about getting orders into how to give my family some of my time.

Cash flow and financial management needs to be left to the professionals once you have made it. If you think running a company is the same as running a hobby that makes money out of your home, think again. You need to know where your money is going and how much. Consider a bookkeeper to start and a good accountant for that yearly, state of the union sit-down. You need to have contingencies in place to manage the cash flow during slow periods in the economy.

When I was a commercial photographer I needed to take on weddings as a revenue stream because commercial work usually slowed down in the summer. It turned out it was a great idea and doubled my business. This allowed me to bring on some good photographers who I could keep busy year-round.

One of the things I see in entrepreneurs who have a steady source of customers is that they start to take things for granted. It's very easy to creep into your business if you are not careful; like the new sports car you dreamed about or the bigger than you need warehouse because it was available. Taking things for granted also means you may slip on your customer service a little and the next thing you know the competition captures him. Blaming the customer is a good excuse that usually follows losing one.

Plan B should be written down somewhere. What the heck will I do if...? If I get that huge monster order do I have a Line of Credit in place, do I have backup part time staff I can call in on short notice? Or can I subcontract work out to professionals I know I can trust? Plan B can be something as important as your exit strategy or as simple as having short cash reserves in place.

The thing entrepreneurs find most appealing about being one is that no day is the same. You are calling the shots and your decisions carry the company forward or in some cases backward. Being in charge can also be your biggest problem unless you actively plan and consider your options.

Pay It Backward CEO's

I was having coffee with some friends the other day talking about some Business deals we were putting together and it occurred to me that at 60 I was the youngest of the group. The other three were CEOs of their own companies and still relished going to work every day. In their late 60's and one in his early 70's none would consider retiring. All had pensions and still earned substantial incomes.

I was reminded of a conversation I had with the former CEO of a leading NGO in Vancouver a couple of years ago. He had been a senior VP at a major bank and had retired early with a substantial pension. When the opportunity to serve as the CEO of the NGO was offered he eagerly accepted it because at 55 he was not ready to retire to the cottage or go fishing. He threw the NGO a zinger when he offered to take a greatly reduced salary.

Why would he do that? He told me that it felt good to give something back to the community and he could afford to because of his pensions. Imagine the ramifications of hiring retired CEOs. With baby boomers accounting for the highest demographic ever, health a non issue with 60 being the new 50 and people remaining active well into their 80's there is a wealth of knowledge that is going to waste.

I've been in interviews for the CEO position of at least two NGOs in the past year. The interviewers were committed volunteers deeply connected to the charity they were involved in. The crux of the interviews invariably turned to my knowledge of the charity's focus; let's say it was diabetes. I asked them if they wanted a professional business person or someone with diabetes. The answer both times was the former but they hired the person with diabetes; another charity doomed to be run by dilettantes.

What if they could have the retired CEO used to earning $250k for their budget of $100k? Would they pass up that knowledge-base to find someone with diabetes, I hope not.

What if, for the first time, agencies, charities, etc. could have expert decision makers running their organization? It is a win/win situation.

What if You Can't Make It as an Entrepreneur - the Intrapreneur

Wikipedia says an Intrapreneur "uses entrepreneurial skills such as innovation, persistence, and risk taking while working as an employee of a large company. For example, a company searches for a new leader with entrepreneurial skills to bring major changes to an under performing division."

Imagine an employee who comes up with innovative ideas for the company and then uses the resources and assistance of the company to bring the ideas to fruition, all for the benefit for the company?

3M is a perfect example of a company who took the efforts of an employee who had a brilliant idea and let him run with it- the guy? – The inventor of Post-it-Notes (Art Fry)!

Do intrapreneurs make good entrepreneurs? What a dilemma! Some people are just plainly long term employees who like the stability of the job, the resources available to them and the company mindset that allows these extraordinary people to work within a corporate structure while maintaining some independence. So the answer to that is no, they make terrible entrepreneurs.

On the other hand... a risk-taking employee given the impetus to take a higher degree of risk may jump the line from dedicated intrapreneurs to entrepreneur and successfully run their own business. Ah, the fine line between an exceptional employee and a great business owner.

I work with 'real' entrepreneurs each and every day. I always look at them and ask myself their chances of success. Boy, it's a crap shoot these days so a failed business doesn't necessarily make them failures. I think an entrepreneur enjoys the thrill of the chase and this fits both intrapreneurs and entrepreneurs.

I'm often told that a lot of businesses prefer a new employee who has been an entrepreneur in their life over a regular employee who comes from a strictly employee background. The theory is that the entrepreneur has the sensitivities of being a business owner and understands what goes into business ownership.

Phew, life is so complicated!

Chapter Fourteen
The Big Exit

Exit Strategies

So you have setup your business, are you going to work at the business until you retire and pass it on to your children? You may have a short term game plan, e.g. get the business up and running like Hotmail did and sell it off quickly for a lot of money and move on to the next business. If you're starting a plumbing business for instance, are you thinking of a long term thing? If you called your business Bob Smith Plumbing & Sons and your kids are in their early teens I guess you are thinking long term.

Your exit plan may include bringing in investors for growth and possible exiting in a period of time. Maybe you have a plan to franchise your business. Planning how you exit your business is just as important as how you start it.

The goal is to maximize the value of your company before converting it to cash, and to minimize the amount of time consumed. These options should be considered an integral part of your business planning.

There are several exit strategies open to a business owner.

You can sell it,

You can bring on a partner and slowly let him take over ownership over time,

You can have a larger company buy you out,

Or you can create a succession plan where you divest of your business over time with a plan usually to family members.

I prefer the scenario when a larger company offers to buy your company for obscene amounts of cash.

Five Reasons Someone Would Want to Acquire Your Company

A client of mine was approached by a foreign company the other day which wants to develop a similar product in my client's territory. The obvious first overture by the big company was to find out how large my client was and determine the appropriate acquisition model. The big company, we will call Xenon, suggested a collaboration where they install their expertise in my client's software and sell it as a more robust package. You can call this the synergy approach where the whole is greater than the sum of the parts.

Xenon had only briefly mentioned the word 'acquisition' but I felt it might be more a problem than my client thought. The more I looked at the scenario that could unfold, the more I wanted to explain to my client what the acquisition model might look like once Xenon had moved into our territory. Xenon had a few reasons to form an alliance then acquire my client's company. Xenon had already captured 50% market share in its own country. They had no where to go except new markets with a similar product base and similar demographics.

Why would a company want to acquire another smaller company? Here are a few considerations to ponder while you try to figure out how much your business is worth to a potential buyer.

To Build a Product

Why would Xenon build a totally new product when they can just buy one with existing customers and proprietary software developed over years? Exactly – a proven product with sales is a better catch than Xenon's product development team trying to redevelop or re-engineering someone's great product, then have their sales team try to market and sell the new product in a foreign market. It's much easier to buy an existing one.

I have a share in a software company that has an app for banking. When we approached a national bank they thought it was amazing but said they already had allocated $20 million to develop their own. Pretty silly comment when our price to them was about 50 cents per customer per month. They still don't have their app created after 4 years.

To Kill the Competition

I love this one because it is diabolical. Sun Tsu would agree in his Art of War. When I was in university an engineering buddy of mine developed a product that increased car engine life many fold. He was approached by an automotive engine company that bought him out before he was even out of university. They proceeded to hide the formula deep in a vault somewhere. Ford didn't want cars that would last forever. They sell cars.

Many software businesses that no longer exist were dismantled this way because it was easier to buy out the little guy and make him disappear to avoid competition down the road.

Priming the Pump of an Existing Sales Channel

Every company needs new clients, so imagine when a big company has pushed each of its distribution channels to the limit. What do they do? They need new products which they can get by acquiring a new company and product line. This gives the established company more fuel in the system and since they are established the new products take on recognized trustworthiness.

Key Employees

A gaming developer client was approached by a big conglomerate to buy his small three guy gaming engine business. A great price was offered and rejected by my client because as part of the deal the owner and his two employees had to work for the new owners and develop programs for him as employees. Although the salaries were great and the picture looked rosy this true entrepreneur said no to the deal.

To Control a Market

My client fits this rationale as well as a couple of the others. When a big company wants to control a market it makes sense to go into a market and buy up complementary businesses that will enhance the big company's offering. It's like Ford Motor Company buying up a parts distribution business. It makes sense and goes to the reason why build a new mousetrap.

When someone approaches you about partnering or alluding about acquiring your business be aware of why they think it's a good acquisition and be ready for the discussion about money. I have clients who have an exit strategy that includes being 'bought out' by a bigger company for millions. It happens!

Are you unsure of your next business move? Ask for Help!

Chapter Fifteen
Give me an Entrepreneur with Heart, Commitment

All my life I've heard the pitches; follow the 'secret', the law of attraction, increase your motivation, find your motivation, find your inner strength, gain self confidence and a plethora of other non tangibles. Oh and let's not forget the warning they give you if you don't buy their snake oil – 'miss this opportunity and you'll be a loser forever'.

I'm telling you forgetaboutit.

I am so sick and tired of listening to the pitches to 'make you the man you always wanted to be and get rich by following my simple techniques to improve your mental state' and other methods to take advantage of the weak and gullible.

I want to deal with winners not losers! I want to be the coach/mentor of an entrepreneur who knows what he wants, is committed and is implementing his dreams. He has the support from family and friends who care – not friends who are enablers. I want clients who can tell the difference between a business plan and a form letter to join a 'find your inner entrepreneur' sales coven.

Mind you I don't have a problem with people who need that sort of stuff but I am not going to work with those people anymore. What did Peter Finch say to the TV masses in the movie Network, "I'm mad as hell and I'm not going to take it anymore"? The excuses, the blame, the guilt and everything else that shrinks and self help 'gurus' dream about are not for me.

Give me an entrepreneur with heart, commitment, guts and who is not afraid to take the steps to be successful and I will lead and/or follow that man to the end and give him support until he tells me to stop.

I truly wish I could sell one of those programs, really. I wish I could get tons of people to send me money to learn how to be your own man, be a success, the eternal optimist and an opportunist.

But hey, what they're selling doesn't come from a self help book or the one hour inspirational lecture or two day workshop. You must own it, possess it already and have the confidence to take it to the next step.

I wish I could sell that type of dream to people but I couldn't live with myself.

I know there are people out there who can size up a product, situation and opportunity and make lots of hay while the sun shines. For the rest of us, we need more than luck. We need systems, a plan, money in place, a focus and good people in place as support and the desire to continue learning or keeping up with changes to your industry.

Learn as much as you can about marketing, accounting, sales strategies, financial administration and setup your systems.

Learning never stops nor should it. I took up photography when I was 12 years old. I was no good but liked the intricacy of the camera and what I could do with it. It wasn't until years later when I took the road to professional photography. I remember the day, June 19, 1977; I had a new camera and was taking pictures of my Dad in Florida while he spoke to a buddy. I was so pleased with myself.

The next day my Dad passed away suddenly. I was heartbroken but comforted by the fact that I had all those photos from the previous night. I developed the film when I got home and found they were all ruined, caused by a switch I had failed to move as I took the pictures.

At that moment I swore that I would learn everything there was; to be the best photographer in Vancouver. I read every single book in the Vancouver Public Library on photography over the next year, all 920 of them - Phew. I didn't become the best photographer in Vancouver but within 5 years I was one of the best.

Talk to people, ask for help and don't think that the lawyer, accountant and consultant are not in your budget. Thinking you can do everything yourself is folly.

Pondering Changing Roles

I was sitting with a client over lunch pondering the different roles I face on a daily basis with my different clients. The Friend works quite well for some. I give advice and they take it as they would from a friend. Oddly, I have friends who won't take my advice.

I play the Bully at times playing my client like a viola hoping to instill some common sense in their brain all the while thinking how various people need diverse methods.

I become the Confidante to the client who is facing doubt and fear hoping like heck I am giving solace to them and a solution to their personal issues.

I share their triumphs and their failures, pat them on the back and slap them on the side of the head when needed.

I'm told I'm very blunt but fair. I tell it like it is and don't often sugarcoat my opinions or the scenario. That doesn't benefit anyone.

The consultant in me gives my client informed statements about their business that, if taken, will make drastic positive change. The coach in me cajoles the client into seeing my point of view with direction and the counselor in me, gives them the tools to make their own informed decision.

I wrote down some things that I do on a regular basis with my clients. I thought it might be fun to put on the back of my business card, but hey, talk about a generalist.

Money Found

Media Produced

Corporations Run

Coaching planned

Budgets followed

Problems identified

Processes Improved

Companies Analyzed

Businesses Managed

Technology Implemented

Business Plans Developed

& Marketing Plans Designed

I love doing what I do!

Check out My Videos on Social Media Marketing & Others on YouTube

My Website at www.GaryBizzo.com

Want to learn more and hear about new opportunities? Join my Mailing List

Our Startup/Small Business Aggregator Authority site www.BizzoBoard.com

Twitter account: @garybizzo

Use the Following Worksheets & Case Studies to get Your Business Going Fast!

Appendices

Bonus eBook:

How to Be a Social Media Rockstar- A Social Media Strategy Checklist

Self Employment Assessment

Biz Planning Worksheet

Biz Checklist

The Business Plan Template

Hello Entrepreneur Survey

Name Brainstorming Session

Action Plan Market Research

Action Plan Permits and Licensing

Survey – Are you ready?

Action Plan – Strategic Alliances

Real Business Case Studies:

Retail, Mobile Flower Shop

Startup, Environmental Technologies/Project Management

Change Management- Graphic services Business

Startup, R&D Invention development

Marketing, Land Development Corporation

Startup, B2B, Food & Beverage

Service Industry

Startup, Distribution, Hospitality

Startup, Health Industry

Growth, Service Industry

Social Media Checklist - How to Be A Social Media Rock Star

It's like any plan you'll ever make. When you devise a social marketing plan you will need to treat it like a well organized plan including goals, time set aside to manage it as an integral part of another plan; it's your marketing plan. I am a firm believer in developing a Business Plan for any venture.

I like to have lists of target 'types' of people who I want to connect to or rather engage. To connect you must understand them. If you are going to utilize Twitter, simply enter a search item in the Search Engine on Twitter and follow people who come up. I like to follow 'entrepreneurs' and we all tend to stick together so about 60% of those I follow will follow me back.

Engage people about important things to you every day in a two way conversation on Twitter for 10 minutes. Engagement may seem like a buzz word but it's a true measure of a social media type to engage in conversation with someone in a meaningful way. It's not good enough to just say "hi how are you doing'. I often click on the person's Twitter name which takes me to their profile instantly. Once there I feel a little more connected to them often because the 'handle' they use on twitter may not have their name but the profile does. When I send a tweet to @CharacterofMan to engage but call him Bob it impresses him because he knows I have gone to the trouble to find out more about him. I now am on the way to having a relationship with this person. I find it amusing when I go to a networking event wearing my own personalized nametag with only my twitter name and a very large QR code. People with whom I may have 'engaged on Twitter come up to me and introduce themselves. It's kind of fun to be able to put a name to a face. I've met some wonderful people that way.

Remember when we used to network in person? Join a social media site once a week and develop it completely. I must belong to about 100 social media sites. I may not be active in that many of them but each one of them has a complete profile of me on them. There's nothing worse than seeing a profile minus a face picture or missing a profile.

Join websites that monitor and track your statistics to know where you are in relation to others like Klout, Dashboard on Blog, etc. Klout is a cool website/tool that gives you stats on people following you on Twitter, the amount of 'real' people you influence and other great stats. Rated from 1-100 depending on your influence with people (meaning do they follow your advice, do they ReTweet your posts, etc.) you can be assured that someone with a rating of over 70 is someone who has consistently given out good information and has a steady following. At this writing mine is 70. Check it out at http://klout.com/garybizzo I use the 'dashboard on my blog to keep abreast of comments on my blog, stats on who is visiting, what part of my blog they are visiting etc. If you're not getting visitors why not? I often send a post on Twitter about a topic I've written on my blog. I call it 'pull' marketing because I'm trying to draw people or pull them to my website. Push marketing on the other hand is when I send them an offer of a book or video for a price.

Unless you really want to mess up or have only 10 followers on your social media site monitor what is being said about you and your business on Google Alerts. I am on a social media site called Foursquare which allows you to check into places, become mayor by having a number of visits, get specials, e.g. restaurant discounts and you can leave comments. I showed a friend and GM of a very large Vancouver Restaurant this website and some of the comments that had been made. Firstly, I was surprised he had not heard of the iPhone app and secondly he was very surprised when I showed him that I was the Mayor of his restaurant and that there were 10 comments about the food and staff. Wow, what an awakening he had when he looked at the bad comments about a certain dish. No one had complained rather they posted them on a social media site for the world to see. You need to keep an eye on things that can affect you personally.

I MUST check my email several times a day on my Smart phone or I will go into convulsions! Answer email ASAP. I have a client who had a message on his phone saying if he didn't answer the phone he was busy and that he only responds to messages at 1pm and 6pm. He had the same message on his email. The result was people didn't want to do business with him because he was not accessible enough in this instant gratification society we now live in. If you're in business, damn well answer your phone and mail immediately.

Pay for one professional photo for all of your Social media and keep it current. This is a no brainer. I asked a friend how to increase my Twitter followers, he told me to drop the suit and tie picture I had in my profile because no one will follow a business guy all suited up. I didn't take his advice and still have at this writing 240,000 Twitter followers*. A professional portrait is inexpensive when you consider all the places you can use it. Heck if you can't afford a really good one go to Sears and use the free one they give you.

If you aren't tech savvy hire someone to develop a professional looking Blog for you. WORDPRESS is very easy to get the hang of for people with limited abilities. I laugh at the prices people pay for websites and blogs today. I used to charge $50,000 for an average website, now the same one can be had for $1500. Blog templates can be purchased for under $200 and are so easy to use because they were designed for the average guy to use it on a daily basis.

Write one blog post once or twice per week on relevant topics, of course this is a guide, often I don't blog for 3 weeks but blog on 3 topics, this keeps the site fresh and keeps bringing people back which is your goal. Blogs have taken websites to the next level, interaction and immediacy. If you write interesting pieces on your blog and I'm not talking about what you had for lunch, people will come back another day to see what else you have written. People don't care if your writing is poor as long as you give them content – Content is King! By changing your blog every week, you make it dynamic rather than a website that sits there and does nothing, once it's seen people go, blogs bring people and customers back.

Provide a free offering on your Blog to help you develop a database, use 'aWeber' service to 'capture' these folks and respond to them professionally. Well, duh, you're reading my free offering, if you like it you may come back as a guest or a customer (I hope). Since you have responded to a social media article maybe I can convince you to spend money next time on another product of mine. The good thing is you have 'opted-in' to possibly receive more offerings from me by subscribing to my list. I promise I won't offer you garbage.

If you engage other bloggers and write comments you will generate links, try commenting on 4 per week. I love responding to other people's blogs. I always get a kick out of people putting comments about a blog post – It tells me people are reading it. You should respond to the comment even just to say thanks, but engagement (there's that word again) is always welcome and really good if you have something to contribute.

Be generous to other bloggers and tweeters by RT or comments. Good karma is always the best; if you don't have something nice to say don't write it, it's all about people's opinions and some can create tremendous issues. I commented on Obama in a Tweet and received 800 reply tweets about it and lost 1000 followers in 5 minutes.

This is about engagement and relationships so personally e-mail a Reader. I have met hundreds of people online, many are now friends. I've secured contracts and sold stuff to them too. It all started with a comment, a tweet or a post.

Check Twitter often. Again the immediacy of Twitter is awesome. A tweet was the first news about the death of Michael Jackson, Obama claims he owed a lot to Twitter for getting elected President in 2008.

Send out around 10 tweets per day on interesting relevant topics. I rarely send out stupid tweets, like how's the weather in LA, who cares. I refer people to other businesses I know and love, I send people interesting quotes and always send loads of info on business and entrepreneurs, my particular favorite topic.

Some days are higher traffic days than others. Send out more tweets (about 15-20) on Tuesday, Thursday and Friday. I was amazed at this. Then one of my social media stars told me college students are more often online those days and around 4- 6 pm. Stats can tell you when to post info to get to the people you want to target. If I want to reach people in the UK, I post early morning Vancouver time, I also know China is 13 hours ahead.

ReTweet at least 5 Posts from Other Blogs, be generous to others and it will come back to you. The generosity vibe is very important. If you say something nice about someone they will befriend you and tell 4 others about you. That's guerrilla marketing for sure.

Each day 'Follow' 100 people who are interesting or relevant to you, who share your goals or are in your industry. I love entrepreneurs, I manage 120 startup businesses a year and all my friends are self employed. I also love business that's why so many people follow my business tweets. Keep it relevant and interesting so good people will enjoy following you and will also tell others

Once a week 'UnFollow' 100 people, who don't follow you on Twitter, you may not fit their demographic or interest level. I often go through my 'followers' and pull out people who obviously I have nothing to share with, e.g. porn stars, huge corporations, religious zealots. It's my opinion and I want to reach the right people

Don't follow more than you follow on Twitter. There are lots of reasons for this one of which is Twitter will think you are spamming people or are a machine. Your statistics will be drastically improved if you keep a reasonable ratio of followers and those you follow.

I like to check FaceBook daily, have new posts sent to your primary email address. I really use Facebook for two things, to have fun connecting with friends and to promote other peoples businesses. I don't consider it really a business tool but it sure does allow me to connect with friends instead of calling them or sending emails. It keeps you engaged so you don't lose friends

Why would you acknowledge friends birthdays on FaceBook, it's announced every day on your page. I can tick a box and someone gets a nice happy birthday wish from me, how pathetic if we can't take 5 seconds to acknowledge someone on a special day. Engage, engage and engage again.

Be adventurous, join groups and fan pages on FaceBook, Groups on LinkedIn. I must admit joining tons of groups dilutes the time I can spend on more important things but sometimes the groups are cool and interesting and I get notifications each time someone writes a comment on them, often these comments are useful in my business. It also allows me an opportunity to resend info to others it may benefit

Are you on LinkedIn? You should be. Check LinkedIn every 2 days for new email, people wanting to join. I get a notice every time someone wants to join my LinkedIn page. I am a LION, a Linked In Open Networker. This means I will accept all who want to be in my network because I feel networking is really important and by having a large following I can meet exceptional people. I met and worked for the Mayor of Mexico City because of a LinkedIn contact and query by him.

Accept LinkedIn requests to follow you if they make sense to you. You may not be the social butterfly I am so accept contact requests if they have some relevance to your job or business. 90% of North American Recruiters are on LinkedIn and go there first to source new 'hires'.

Add business card emails into LinkedIn once a week. It's part of your database. I meet a lot of interesting business people in my Meetups and other places, why not include them in your database, they have given you their card so they must be interested in hearing from you. If I have their card they are fair game to be invited to join my LinkedIn family.

Go to LinkedIn's Q&A section and offer answers to questions. One of the ways to increase your profile is to be an expert. Answering questions posed by other business people if it's your area of expertise will elevate you in the minds of others and draw more people to your website and profile assuming you have an offer on your website.

Read other posts on LinkedIn groups in your area of expertise to remain current.

Go to your iTunes store or whatever you use to source new Apps weekly for your Smart phone. I love my iPhone and the app store. I have about a 100 on my phone and iPad. I have fun stuff but all of the apps are geared to extending my social media reach. I have social media aggregation software, apps to increase my productivity and apps to help me connect with others easier.

Develop a QR code for your Business Card, don't know what that is? Check it out. It's like a bar code that has an incredible amount of information on including access to your website, all of your contact information and an abundant of things important for you to get out to your customers, friends or people you meet at a tradeshow. I have a QR code printed on the back of my business card. A person I meet can quickly scan the code on a Smart Phone and be taken directly to my website. An incredible feat if we are standing together at a tradeshow. By the way it's free.

Start your Own Meetup for $65 and send out invites to join. If you are an entrepreneur in Vancouver near my office you can attend about 45 networking meetings called meetups spread throughout the week. You can setup your own group or join an existing one in your area of interest. I have a realtor client who joined a realtor Meetup. He likes to chat about real estate and finds it helpful, if he was hoping to get a listing or sell a house he may have opted to go to an entrepreneur Meetup or a builder Meetup. Check out http://meetup.com.

Make sure your Blog/Website is Search Engine Optimized (SEO). I just talked to a new client today who only ranks on Google when you type in his complete website address, nothing else. Putting good money into a blog or website and then not promoting it even from the most basic standpoint seems useless to me, again you don't need to spend a lot of money look around for a good SEO person and watch your traffic improve.

Chardonnay Effect- OK folks so here is the clincher. I love Chardonnay wine, that invigorating beverage at the end of a tough day at the office. How many times have you wished you had not sent an email to someone or posted a tweet to someone then realized you must look like an idiot or it might come across different than you intended? OK, now add 2 or 3 glasses of wine to your judgment and see what happens, your engagement will turn into a nightmare trust me- been there and done that. Send it tomorrow when clearer heads prevail. The most important thing about social media for me is to devote as much time as you can or feel comfortable doing and have fun.

I hope you have felt I have given you some valuable information up to now. I've been told I am a very clever guy and even an expert in social media.

This item is one of my biggest lessons for you - PROTECT YOUR PASSWORDS AT ALL COSTS. December of 2011 after a night of celebrations and a little tired I logged into my Twitter account and was hit by a notice asking me if I wanted to be Verified as a Twitter user. It's like being validated by Twitter for being well known, possessing huge numbers or being a celebrity. In my tiredness I immediately said yes and signed into an official looking form asking me for my User Id and Password. I gave those two as requested and within one measly minute lost 160,000 Twitter followers.

The form was a fake, the Verification was a 'phishing' trip designed to appeal to my ego and give up my account. The perpetrator was a 14 year old sociopath from Los Angeles. It wasn't hard to figure out who he was even though he changed the name of my account and set up a new one for me with no followers in it. Twitter refused to do anything because the first thing he had done after changing the password was to change the email address. Twitter identifies the account to the email address. Out of luck! I felt like crap for about 2 months, went to a lawyer, the FBI and the CIA – believe it or not I did. They all had empathy but Twitter held all the cards along with my 14 year old perp.

I picked up myself in March and embarked on a new social media campaign. At this writing I have around 230,000 on my second iteration. **FULL SPEED AHEAD!**

Self-Employment Assessment Test

Use this Self-Employment Assessment Test to determine if you have what it takes to be self-employed.

Please note: As you answer each question, do it quickly. Don't give any question too much thought; just go with your first, gut-level reaction. Answer with a "yes," a "no," or a "?" and at the end of the 25 questions, you'll see how to score yourself.

Are you a quick learner?

Are you self-motivated?

Are you healthy – emotionally and physically?

Do you possess an extra amount of common sense?

Do you love to learn new tasks and ideas?

Do you have a high tolerance for risk?

Do you enjoy doing sales?

Do you constantly like to meet new people?

Can you juggle multiple tasks and responsibilities at the same time?

Do you regularly set and accomplish personal goals?

Are you willing to sell your product or service?

Do you have a spouse or friend who will take an interest in the business?

Can you live with high levels of uncertainty?

Are you resilient?

Do you make good decisions quickly?

Are you good with money?

Do you love to work?

Do you thrive on competition?

Do you have will-power and self-discipline?

Are you a good leader?

Do you get things done on time?

Can you live without an income until your business reaches break-even?

Do you have skills and passion for the business you're considering?

Are you resourceful?

Are you willing and prepared to work long hours in the beginning?

Business Planning Worksheet

Before you go into business you should attempt to learn as much about the business (and yourself!) as possible. This worksheet-- if you actually fill it out and answer all questions honestly--will help you collect and evaluate essential information about yourself and the business you would like to start. While it won't give you all the facts you need to determine if you should pursue your business idea, it will help you answer some very fundamental questions and help you identify possible pitfalls.

List the reasons you want to go into business for yourself

Are you willing to work long hours even if this business doesn't make money immediately?

Have you ever worked in a similar business?

Have you ever worked as a foreman or manager?

Have you taken any business courses in school?

Describe what you plan to sell in one or two sentences?

Describe your typical customer:

Consumer sales

Age

Sex

Family income:

Geographic location:

Buying habits:

Frequency of product use:

Business Sales

Industry:

Purchasing/decision maker:

How big is the market?

Is the market growing, static, or declining?

How much of the market can you reach?

In what geographic areas are those kinds of businesses and/or consumers located?

How will you get your products or services to them, or how will they (customers) get to you?

Who are your competitors?

How well are they doing?

How will you distinguish your products or services from theirs?

Price

Performance

Quality

Strength

Speed

Size; color

Other

Is there really a need for another business like the one you are planning to start?

How will you advertise your business?

Who will prepare your ads?

Where can you get help with your ads?

How do other businesses like the one you are considering get customers?

Do you know how to price the products or services you plan to sell?

Do you know what other businesses are charging for products and services like those you plan to sell?

What have you done to find out what your potential customers really want to buy?

If you will be selling products, do you have a system devised for tracking inventory and determining when to reorder?

Where will you get your stock if you are selling a product?

Who will actually do the selling? You or a salesperson?

Do you have any sales training, or have you studied books on salesmanship?

Do you like selling?

How much money do you have now to put into this business?

How much money do you need to start this business?

Where will you get the rest of the money you need to start this business? (List sources and amounts)

How much credit will you be able to get from suppliers (people you will have to buy goods or services from)?

How much money do you expect to make per year from this business (salary and profit on investment)?

What is the minimum amount of money you need per year to meet living expenses?

Have you discussed business loans with a banker or an accountant?

Will you need a partner to supply money or business know-how?

If you will need a partner, do you know someone who would be appropriate and with whom you are sure you could get along?

Have you investigated the pros and cons of working on your own (sole proprietor), with a partner, or as a corporation?

Have you discussed your plans with a lawyer?

Are most businesses in your community doing well?

Are other businesses like the one you want to start doing well in your area?

Are other businesses like the one you want to start doing well in the rest of the country?

Where will you find employees if you need them?

Are other businesses in you area having difficulty finding qualified help?

What salary will you have to pay to get reliable help?

How will you train your employees?

Do you know how long it normally takes to get paid in your line of business?

Will you accept credit cards?

Have you investigated the requirements of credit card companies and the benefits and drawbacks of accepting credit cards?

Could you make more money working for someone else?

Are you sure you will have the support of your family?

Do you read trade journals or other sources of information about new ideas and products in your field?

Biz Check List

Here is a checklist of the basic areas you need to cover before opening your business:

Write a Business Plan. Choose & Register a Business Name

Decide on the Legal Form for the Business

Set the Price for Your Product or Service

Determine the Financing You Will Need and How You Will Get It

Set up Other Professional Relationships and Strategic Alliances

Meet Legal Requirements for Operating a Business

Get Licenses and Permits

Set up a Relationship with a Lawyer, if needed

Set up a Relationship with a Banker

Obtain Office Space, Equipment and Suppliers

Plan for Risk & Insurance

Set up Record-keeping Systems

Set up a Financial Management System

Develop a Marketing Plan

Hire Employees

Develop a Day-to-Day Managerial Plan

Each of these areas needs careful consideration if your business is to become a reality and prosper. There are resources available if you search business sites if you have a problem understanding the headers.

Business Name Brainstorming

List three ideas based on the products or services you plan to provide (e.g., children's clothing, custom menu design, aromatherapy products).

List three ideas based on your special niche (e.g., affordable children's special occasion clothes, exclusive designs for the small restaurateur, aromatherapy for the office environment).

List three ideas based on your special niche (e.g., affordable children's special occasion clothes, exclusive designs for the small restaurateur, aromatherapy for the office environment).

List three ideas combining a favorite theme with your special niche: (e.g., Tea Party, children's party clothes, Table for Two menu designs, The Tranquil Desk aromatic office products).

After you've decided which name you like best, ask yourself a few important questions.

Have you said it aloud to make sure it's easily understood and pronounced?

(Has it passed muster with your family? Have you had a friend call to see how it sounds

over the phone?)

Have you checked the internet to make sure the same or a similar name is not already listed?

Have you checked with your local business authority to make sure the name is available?

Business Plan Structure – Start Up Operations

Covering Page

Executive Summary

Content Page

Mission Statement

Vision Statement

Personnel Plan

Description On And Particulars Of The Company

Organizational Structure

Who's Who, Job Description, Expectations and Remuneration For Various Positions

Company Policies

Payroll Budget

Marketing Plan

Situational Analysis

Overview Of The Industry

Opportunities

Threats

Internal Audit

Business Model (Concept)

Strengths

Weaknesses

Market

Bases for Market Segmentation

Market Targeting

Market Positioning

Competition

Description On The Top Five (5) Direct/Indirect Competitors

Competition Matrix

Anti-competitor Campaign

Strategies and Tactics

Objectives

Product

Pricing

Place

Promotion

People

Marketing Budget

Financial Plan

Summary

Start Up Budget

Cash Flow Forecast

Pro Forma Income Statement

Projected Balance Sheet

Break-even Analysis

Notice to Readers

Action Plan

Monthly Milestones For The Coming 12 Months

Action Matrix

Risk Management / Contingency Plan

Others

Conclusion

Appendix

Supporting Documents

Raw Research Data

Pictures of Promotional Material And Samples

Others

Market Research Action Plan

What is Your Product Niche?

Who is the Competition using Google Search?

Is Your Product or Service Defensible Against Competition?

Have You Confirmed the Name for Your New Business by Google and Government Regulator?

Have You Confirmed Your Demographics?

Based on Demographics Have you identified a Location?

While Considering the Location Conduct an Independent Survey by Watching the Traffic personally for one Day?

Put Together a Competition Matrix of Your Top Competitors and Compare Your Offering to Each

Have You Compared Your Pricing to Your Competition

Have You Researched Suppliers (if applicable) both locally and outside Your Area?

Do You Know How Much Money You Need to Start and Run for 6 Months?

Permits and Licensing Action Plan

Call City Hall and Ask about setting up a Business License

Research what if any sales tax you need to have for your particular type of business

Call your government regulators and apply for a sales tax

Find out if you need any other permits by Google search, e.g. Flower shop, Vancouver, permits needed

Are you using your vehicle for your business? Do you have proper insurance?

Do you need a building permit?

Action Plan – Are You Ready & Organized Enough?

I am not surrounded by paper piles – my work environment is clear and clutter free.

I have a filing system so that I can easily find important papers.

I always follow up with clients and potential clients when I say I will.

I have important financial data available and know exactly my income and expenses.

I effectively manage my monthly cash flow.

My emails are organized and my in box is not overflowing with unread emails.

If a client expresses an interest in working with me, I have a clear system in place to sign them up for a strategy session.

I have an opt-in box on EVERY page of my website.

I have a free giveaway on my website that I offer in exchange for my visitor's name and email address.

I use a list management service to send out my newsletter/ezine.

I publish my newsletter/ezine on a regular (i.e. weekly/monthly) basis.

I get at least 100 new subscribers every month.

I have a system in place for re-purposing my newsletter articles.

My voice mail promotes my business/free giveaway to callers.

I have clients who are interested in working with me and have had to put them on a waiting list.

I offer a range of services from free to expensive and always have something to offer clients.

I have a vast library of articles that I could collate into an information product.

I have a Signature Information Product that repackages my expertise into a home-study format.

I am fully utilizing the power of auto responders to follow up with my clients and customers and leverage my time.

I am delegating my work and have at least one team member in place.

Action Plan - Hello Entrepreneur

Interview' at least 3 entrepreneurs that may be friends, strangers or someone you know from doing business with them (please no husbands or wives, that's cheating). I want you to ask them the following questions:

What was the biggest challenge in starting up their business?

What type of problems did they encounter that they hadn't anticipated

What kind of support did they wish they had when they were starting out?

When did they feel they were 'over the hump'?

Did their vision of the business change at all over the course of the first year?
What would they do differently if they could do it over?

Action Plan - Strategic Alliances

List 5 powerful influencers you have already in your immediate network who can help move your business forward.

List suppliers you deal with or will deal with in the future.

List 5 group networking events you attend or would like to attend every month, e.g. Meetup, BNI.

Visualize and list 5 possible complementary businesses who may be a match for your business, e.g. a realtor if you are landscaper.

Action Plan – Unique Selling Point (USP)

Based on the USP's discussed in this video, name the top 5 reasons someone should buy from you.

Make a list of your top 5 competitors big or small and compare your top 5 reasons against theirs.

How are you different from your competitors enough for a customer to buy from you?

If you already have customers/clients conduct a survey and ask them why they like buying your product or service and compare it to what you thought was your Unique selling proposition

How is your competition using their USP?

Put yourself in your customer's shoes. If you have great food and think that is your USP, is there something else that you may be missing?

Based on your USP create a psychologically oriented customer acquisition campaign.

Drop into 3 competitor's places of business and check out not only what they sell but how they sell it.

If you are really brave try asking a few of the customers after they leave the premises what they like and dislike about the competitors' products and services.

The Marketing Plan – An Outline

Your Marketing Plan needs to be relevant, prioritize your opportunities, able to utilize your resources and be actionable.

Market Research

Who, what, when, where and why.

Positioning

Define your clearly defensible position in the market

Your pricing must meet client demands and expectations

Strategies and Tactics

What are your strategies?

E.g. Guerrilla – investing energy versus money in unconventional methods

How will you implement them?

What are your expected results?

Your Timelines

All of your Strategies

What technical operations are required?

Action plan

Metrics

How will you measure your success?

Follow-up to your strategies

How to measure your results:

Identifying

Quantifying

Qualifying

Justifying

Tying the Marketing Plan to the Business Plan

Don't work at the marketing plan as if it is in a vacuum

Get input from other stakeholders

Your Checklist

Who are you trying to reach?

What are their needs and priorities?

How can you provide effective quality service?

How are you going to inform the market effectively?

How can you do things better?

How can the company become your client's first choice?

Building Your Brand

How Can You Differentiate Yourself from the Competition?

How good are you on a scale of 1-10?

How good are you compared to the competition?

How good does the market think you are?

How good do the customers think you are?

How good do you rate your own sales ability?

How well do you speak?

How well do you transfer your message?

How well do you bring new ideas to the customer?

How well do you close the deal?

How well do you follow up?

How well do you differentiate yourself?

How well do you create relationships?

How well do deliver value?

How well do you help your customers profit from the use of your product or service?

How well do you build your own self-development knowledge?

Going deeper:

How good are you compared to your competition?

How often do you win when you go up against them? The competition isn't just the enemy they are an indicator.

How good does the market think you are?

What is their impression of you as a person? Do they even know you exist? What impact have you had on the market? What's the big picture of you in the market? For you to be able to sell people must know who you are.

How good do your customers think you are?

This is your 'brand', your reputation, your success, your next sale and your referral.

Insight: Figure out why you haven't reached 10

Hindsight: Self discovery will reveal why, but you must be honest with yourself

Foresight: Once you know the last two grab your bootstraps and make a plan to get ahead. Your personal brand is the most important thing you have. Sales people have a million reasons for bad sales but if you 'brand' yourself properly you will have no excuses.

Case Studies

I produced several Case Studies based on over 120 competencies for my Certification as a Certified Business Counselor at Acadia University. The following are 10 real Case Studies on different operational problems facing real-life entrepreneurs. (Names have been changed to protect their privacy)

Case Study Number 1

Startup, Retail Mobile Flower Shop

Name: Gary C. Bizzo, APEC CBC

Client: TK

Length of Intervention: 40 hours

Location: Bizzo Management Group, Office, Vancouver

Stage in Business: Startup

<u>Background</u>

An existing client (TK) called my office to apply for a Canadian Youth Business Foundation loan for those under 35 years of age. The client has taken the Self Employment program for 10 weeks and with my help has produced a business plan that is also required for the loan. She started a mobile (cart) Flower shop in the lobby of the busiest skytrain station in Vancouver.

Her business plan (BP) indicates a strong understanding of the business from an operational standpoint but her financials suggested she might require some more help. She will have to do some more marketing as her business plan initially was for a more conventional retail space Flower shop. Her product mix is very unconventional as well in that she intends to follow an Asian product model and introduce a new flower product to Canada.

Specifics of counseling objectives

Determine the client's eligibility for funding under Canadian Youth Business Foundation (CYBF) per FICO, references and with an analysis from a staff assessment team composed of 2 business coaches

Because of the loan process we will assist her in setting goals in terms of what to do for the lender to secure the loan and a goal setting session for post loan to mitigate risk and help her get the most from her loan of $30,000

Assess the client in revising an existing marketing plan, revising the financials for a 2 year proforma and develop a new start-up budget

Assist the client to negotiate a lease agreement with the Skytrain authority so that it is beneficial to the client

Assist her in finding a business mentor who can support her while she is on the loan program

Process and skills used

Rapport Building -I have a counseling office setup next to my office where I met TK for the first and subsequent counseling meetings. I have a relaxed setup with a round table to facilitate casual meetings so the client can feel we are in a collaborative environment. I began the meeting by offering coffee and chatting about nothing in particular. We gradually moved on to some discussion about her experiences in my program and finally after she seemed relaxed we spoke of the business and the reason for her visit. As we chatted I told her my colleague Ray would be available at any time to help her with any financial (spreadsheet) questions as that was his expertise. I took her to Ray's office and introduced her to him.

At the first meeting I explained the process of the actual loan inc. interest rates, FICO, Equifax and BDC participation as a second lender. I explained the need for her to have a financial plan that would reflect the use of monies, adequate money for marketing and how a backup financial plan might be useful. I gave her numerous forms and went over them with her including the referee forms, guarantee form, and helped her get through a complicated online application process and online forms.

In order to facilitate the meeting with structure, I used the APEC-IBIZ visuals to determine what I intended to cover with TK. The assessment was helpful to give me a starting point in discussions that were of a high priority on TK's mind and agenda.

<u>Advocate with/for Client</u>- Once TK completed the application and put together all the loan documents I had 2 independent assessors check the plan and the financials and took her application to CYBF where I championed her to their committee

<u>Use Audio Visual Aids</u> The CYBF group has produced a very effective audio visual DVD that describes how the process of securing financing works and provides an overview of financing a business. I went over the presentation video and PowerPoint with TK as an intro to the banking process.

<u>Manage Time</u>- Over the course of several weeks we developed a plan to work on her financials, fulfilled the requirements for the loan and made a 'game plan' with strategies for a seamless operation of her business. Our strategy was to provide specific times for a maximum of 90 minutes over thirteen weeks where we would discuss the issues she had laid out in our preliminary meeting. We had defined the issues and prior to each weekly meeting she would send me an agenda for us to follow. After the meeting I would summarize what I understood we had discussed and forward the summary in an email to help keep her on track.

<u>Perform Location Planning</u>- While the client has a general idea of her proposed flower shop location we brainstormed and did some demographic and psychographic analysis together to come up with a 'killer' location. Our discussions centered around a mall location as she thought a mobile cart might be a good way to start. In our discussion it became apparent that the malls were oversaturated by mobile carts and her business could be lost in the milieu.

I asked TK why she felt the possible locations were more or less appropriate for her product to be sold. Her product is a very small bouquet of flowers easily carried in its own designer paper bag. She explained that her friends found the flowers very appealing and they had enthusiastically supported her to setup the business. I asked her where people similar to her friends might congregate and she identified the busiest skytrain feeder terminal in Vancouver, Granville Skytrain station. I helped her identify the traits her friends possessed and we worked on developing a profile of her customers. She felt the profiles were young persons, mainly female who took the inexpensive transit system to work, who had an office job and liked to see flowers on their desk which were inexpensive and easy to carry. When she explained the incredible numbers of people using the skytrain at 90,000 per day from her location she thought of another demographic; those leaving the office, young men taking a small gift home to girlfriends, wives of parents.

Assist Client in Self Assessment – TK's resume indicated that she had not only been a volunteer in several organizations in her community but held executive positions in these organizations. I asked her if these positions included supervisory experience and/or financial management functions. She indicated they did and that she had learned a great deal about dealing with governments/people of differing personalities as well as finance from these positions. She quickly realized that these experiences could be extrapolated to her current self employment. In subsequent meetings TK exhibited a new found sense that she had done work in the past that was relevant to her new business and our meetings took on a more confident and more directed approach. I think reaching back to past experience and accomplishments was a turning point in out relationship.

Assess Previous Experience- We went through her resume and it was clear her skills learned while abroad in Japan would assist her to provide a new and innovative product to the Canadian market. She has training in floral arrangement but in a different culture (Japan). Being a Canadian born Japanese she has strong roots in Vancouver and knows the Canadian market having worked in retail.

Demonstrating Empathy -In our first conversation, TK had expressed concern that setting up her business might be very expensive. This had been a concern of mine as well considering her idea was unique and the economy was not doing very well. Through our conversation she told me her worry was really not a huge concern because her fiancée was a senior executive at a grand hotel in Vancouver and had considerable assets. Her concern was mainly independence thus the desire for a loan. I pointed out that to have her fiancée as a safety net must be very reassuring to her.

Assess Risk-taking potential – We went over the executive summary and the business plan and discussed what issues may arise in her new business and what she might do in terms of controlling risky business practices, economic downturns and employee issues. She had a section in her BP about Risk Management and had laid out a clear understanding of what issues she may encounter. We discussed employee issues, e.g. fraud because of the nature of flowers having a short shelf life, controlling hours of work if she was not at the 'mobile shop' and other employment issues, i.e. WCB, taxes.

We discussed how owning a business has more than financial considerations. We talked about the risk to relationships particularly since she had recently become engaged. I helped her realize that timing is an important issue and that her decisions may require joint discussions with her fiancée. In our next meeting she told me she had a long conversation with her fiancée about those issues and he was 100% behind her.

As for the personnel issues she talked about friends who could help cover shifts while she got her feet wet and while she fine tuned her operations manual. Unlike some persons who are fearful of hiring employees she admitted that she wanted the business to be fully in her control first and procedures tested by her before she hired even part time people.

Assessing client commitment, Expectations and family support. – We discussed how securing the loan would impact how she would do business but could become a burden if sales were not as expected. By going through her financials we assessed that with a conservative approach she could manage to cover her expenses easily. Her new fiancée is fully behind her with some business expertise and has offered more money if needed. She has indicated her planning for this has been on her mind for 5 years since she returned from Japan and that she had been slowly working towards the goal since. Based on TK's BP her expectation is conservative only in terms of the financial returns, she has sought and secured one of the premium sales spots in Vancouver. We discussed how her enthusiasm must be tempered with the following of both her BP and her Action plan.

Assist Client in Goal Setting -TK and I had developed short term goals for each meeting with a larger goal at the end of each month to attain. Her long range goals are connected with her fiancée and raising a family. To that end she put a lot of effort into the Procedures/Operational Manual she was developing so that she could create not only a manual for staffing but could create a structure that would be able to be franchised as a turnkey operation. In her discussions with the landlord, she had expressed interest in opening up other locations on the rapid transit system and received assurances that she could have first right of refusal and/or could open stores at her discretion

Assess Client's willingness to learn – I first met the client when she applied to the SUCCESS Self Employment program to startup her business. We explored the 48 week program and she told me her strengths and weakness from a SWOT analysis she has done on her own. She was anxious to get into the marketing and in particular the finance workshops. She was accepted into the program and did attend 8 weeks of full time instruction. Her contributions to the class gave her a different perspective in the running of her business.

TK has since finished my program and continues to attend seminars and workshops that I present and that are open to past participants. She asked to accompany me to Vancouver Board of Trade seminars and meetings which I am pleased to do.

Assess Client's decision making skills/ Assess Client's Research Skills - When TK approached us with her business idea of either a full retail flower shop or a mobile in a mall she had amassed a lot of info on similar operations around the world. When faced with options of where to open her shop she had to make quick decisions on whether to option a lease knowing finances would be a consideration and a loan would be needed for her to do the business completely on her own. She had to apply for the lease without knowing if she had the money. She then had to meet with me and a designer to come up with the configuration for her unique mobile flower shop. Given options, she made concrete decisions with the help of an action plan.

She had done extensive market research which included location scouting and location intelligence in Tokyo when she determined her unique idea may 'fly or die' in Vancouver. Through her research she sourced the materials needed for her flower business, e.g. special bags, containers to China and Japan and has arranged to import these in bulk from 2 locations. Importing product is a very complicated procedure and she has worked with me in developing a procedure manual of sorts to accomplish this.

Assess Client negotiating skills– TK was a bit apprehensive when she first discussed a new lease with one of the toughest and largest corporations in Vancouver, Skytrain. We discussed some possible scenarios and she came up with an offer she would make to them at her next meeting. Skytrain is a transportation business and real-estate is a necessary problem in their mind and their take it or leave it attitude is reflected in their leasing contracts. TK not only secured a good lease beneficial to her but secured options on other skytrain stations that will keep her competition at bay.

Outcomes

Assist client in conducting a situational analysis and determine location- TK conducted a situational analysis which gave her direct insight into her clients buying habits and which location would best provide access to these clients. She has since signed a lease on the premier location in the city with options for other locations that are similar on an exclusive deal

Assist client in developing an action plan – With the development of a very strong business plan and ongoing workshops at SUCCESS, TK developed a comprehensive action plan that is serving as a guide and has clearly defined her goals for the operation of her business for the next year.

Client negotiating skills- We helped TK develop the skills necessary to make an informed decision about risk and helped her parlay that into a no-nonsense approach when dealing with her landlord which resulted in a fair arrangement for both sides

Clients decision making- We helped TK formulate her own decisions based on sound research and helped her tap into existing skills she didn't know she possessed.

Financing her business- Through our counseling we helped her develop a good understanding of the loan process and she successfully received a $30k loan and was assigned a mentor by the funder.

Case Study Number 2

Startup, Environmental Technologies/Project Management

Name: Gary C. Bizzo, APEC CBC

Client: X Corp (Client- MG)

Length of Intervention: 60 hours

Location: Various Locations, Vancouver

Stage in Business: Startup (incorporated August 15th, 2008)

Background

     The Managing Director of an unincorporated company had called me on August 1st at my home office from a referral he had found on the professional networking website, www.LinkedIn.com. He indicated that he was going to incorporate a business in Winnipeg that would be a Project Management business utilizing Canadian technologies. He would be working on environmental issues in Mexico in cooperation with senior Mexican officials in Mexico City as well as Guadalajara and 27 other communities in an effort to provide Cdn. Environment technologies to those jurisdictions. He (MG) pointed out that he needed a 'man on the ground' in Canada who knew business issues, the government regulations, culture and could help negotiate contracts between Canadian high technology companies in Toronto, Montreal and buyers in Mexico.

     Because the technologies were considered unproven outside Canada, the Mexican government would not provide contracts or any funding sources at all. The Winnipeg business needed to find upfront investment money in order to develop several prototypes from a Montreal supplier. Once the technology was proven the Mexican government would be on track and place orders in the millions. A second serious concern was that the next President of Mexico (heir apparent) would be using this technology as one of his platforms in the next federal election and any deliberations with those involved had to be very discrete.

I needed to identify possible risks for the stakeholders, help the client create a Cdn. Corp. very quickly, help him with a business plan as well as help to broker a deal that would be a revolutionary milestone in Mexico's attempt to promote environmental sustainability. The task seemed daunting but the client showed a commitment and trust in me by flying into Vancouver from Manitoba for a meeting.

Specifics of counseling objectives

1.   Determine the needs of the client in setting up a Canadian company

2.   Assist the client in developing a Canadian presence and act as a liaison to high tech businesses

3.   Assist the client in developing a business plan

4.   Assist in securing venture capital

5.   Process and skills used

Empower Client – The client is a Canadian citizen originally from Madrid and more recently from Mexico who has reached an impasse with suppliers and financial institutions because of poor English and lack of knowledge of Canadian customs, regs, etc. I felt he needed to be empowered so that my involvement in his company would be a short term 'get him on track' scenario and then exit. Empowerment enables my client to recognize his strengths and abilities and perform on his own. It enables him to solve problems in the future on his own and successfully. I felt if he could understand some of the processes, develop his own business plan and feel comfortable he could then deal with the issues and people on his own. His lack of confidence was paralyzing. He also felt some corporate executives were not giving him the respect he deserved as a professional engineer.

<u>Maintain Currency in Technology</u> – I have a very strong Social Media networking system in place that allows people to find me with ease. The client located me through my profile on the professional site www.linkedIn.com I also belong to a LinkedIn group working with Canadian Immigrants which appealed to the client as he is a recent immigrant.

MG and I arranged a meeting at lunch for the next day and he flew in from Winnipeg for the day. I had my netbook with wireless connectivity to the restaurant's high speed internet and we discussed his business, he showed me a PowerPoint presentation and we connected to websites for his suppliers and partners in Mexico City. The client needed a Vancouver presence so I introduced him to Skype and showed him how he could create a Vancouver phone number that forwarded to his Winnipeg office.

<u>Recognizing Limitations/Develop and Maintain Network of Expertise and Support</u>- I am a firm believer in a synergistic approach to counseling and think strong teams can only make the counselor stronger and provide better service to the client. B15 -Finding support for the client began with the introduction through the Canadian Immigrant Magazine group on LinkedIn. I needed the services of a contract lawyer to work on Non Disclosure Agreement's, supplier contracts and incorporation papers. I brought in a CGA to help MG understand the complexities of business financials needed for his business plan. I called in a Virtual office assistant to help setup an office quickly.

<u>Assess Client's Knowledge of Local Regions</u> – Early in our relationship I had to determine what knowledge my client was lacking in terms of cultural, economic and political savvy. In our first meeting over coffee we had exchanged personal information and I had determined that MG had feelings of cultural inferiority brought about by business reaction to him in Canada. He and his family live in a Prairie province not usually inhabited by Mexican immigrants but his sister had moved there some years ago and he wanted to be near family. He admitted that once he had settled in Winnipeg it was clear that location was not right for a high tech corporation with

international implications. MG assumed people would line up to become involved in his project and was amazed when investors initially failed to materialize. I helped MG consider and then open a Vancouver satellite office.

Manage Meetings/Identified Cultural Differences –My client had expressed concern about how to setup meetings with his 4 levels of stakeholders. I helped him work out an agenda, prioritize some issues and went over presentation skills including PowerPoint that would accommodate his heavily accented English. Next we setup a conference/video connection between his partner in the Mexico City office, the Mayor of Mexico City in his office, an interpreter in Toronto, and suppliers in Montreal and Toronto.

The problem of possible misunderstandings was a concern so each teleconference included notes taken by an assistant and then emailed to all parties. Any discrepancies or questions were dealt with immediately. One of two possible investors that we met was from Shanghai. The meeting between a Chinese man who likes to feel out his possible business partners over several social meetings, the Toronto supplier who wanted answers immediately and the Mexican who liked to make decisions quickly but liked to do so over several beers needed a moderator. I kept the meetings on track and worked toward consensus understanding each person's cultural differences.

Meetings were also arranged in person in Vancouver. The client felt much more relaxed in a one on one situation and in a relaxing restaurant. I learned a lot about how the Spanish like to conduct business.

Listen – From my first couple of meetings I realized I had to listen very carefully to catch each nuance and accented word uttered by my client. I had to avoid cultural colloquialisms making sure the client understood each word. After each conversation I would write a synopsis and email him. By taking my time to listen to every word I feel I built a level of trust that made my client more comfortable and more open to assisting him.

<u>Communicate in Writing</u> – As discussed the verbal conversations had to be followed up in writing to avoid possible confusion. Working as an editor to my client, using my knowledge of rules and composition, I reworked proposals and assisted in the development of the business plan. I worked on bringing out his ideas on a PowerPoint presentation which turned out to be a good method to get his point across to a group of angel investors while maintaining his confidence level.

<u>Identify Channels of Communication and Authority</u> – When I had met MG, I quickly found out that he was the managing director but lacked complete authority over many decisions. He was the sole owner of the Cdn. Corporation but part of a bigger picture. Channels of communication refer to the medium used to convey information and we used everything at our disposal to connect sender to receiver. As noted before we utilized Skype for intercity telephone service, video conferencing, teleconferencing with interpreters, personal meetings, formalized suit and tie meetings with professionals and angel investors. In the latter we had to follow a 'pitch' format much like Dragon's Den (on CBC). Roles blurred and sometimes I was asked o take on a more active role representing MG when language became a problem. We developed a very close business relationship in a very short time.

<u>Negotiate</u> – Starting a small business requires constant negotiations. In this case I sourced the Vancouver offices and rather than negotiate the terms myself, I gave tips to MG on what would be discussed at a meeting with the landlord, how to structure the offer and what would be a final consensus to his benefit. The negotiations included working on securing angel investment money. Each negotiation big or small required lots of planning on what was acceptable, bottom line and workable. I reminded MG to be prepared to listen even more carefully and to be ready for compromise so he was prepared with prices, exit strategies he could live with and money he could part with for investment. I reminded told him to remember his cultural differences and leave his ego at the door. MG was prepared when he entered negotiations to offer and expect commitment.

<u>Development of a Business Plan/Assess Business Knowledge/</u>
<u>Source Financing</u> – When I was retained by the client it was clear my
job would be to help him deal with Cdn. Laws, regulations and
customs as well as helping him develop a business plan. I think he
originally wanted me to write the plan but I pointed out to him that I
needed to take some time to understand the highly technical project
and since he was the Engineer it made sense for him to write the plan
under my guidance.

I developed a simple template that provided MG questions
which he would answer then remove the questions (like Business Plan
Pro software). It became clear that he was trying to manage the
business side of the project and he was the more business-oriented
part of his Mexican-based team.

It became necessary for me to help him understand the
production of a business plan. I helped him think in engineering terms
so he could relate to the process. He picked up the concepts quickly
with this metaphor and worked well with my template. I developed
parts of the plan with simplistic headers and portions that asked the
necessary questions in an easily understood way. Any areas he had
trouble with e.g. a SWOT analysis I gave him examples and let him
come up with his own answers. There was a lot of money involved in
this project so his proposal/business plan had to be accurate, well
prepared, well written and had to stand the scrutiny of investors and
Directors of the company. It also had to act as a guide for him to
continuing to develop the business after I left the contract.

My client was naïve about financing and had been preparing to
secure conventional bank loans with his home as collateral to finance
the business even though he was a minority shareholder in the
corporation. I counseled him on the reasons why this manner of
financing may be flawed. I went over different options such as CIDA
(which we found out did not support Cdn. /Mexican trade any longer),
SR& ED money to recoup the prototyping he needed for his project
(and had already spent), and angel investment. He had initially told
me they had done the friends and family round of financing and had

raised enough to setup the corporation and had a 6 month operating budget.

Develop Awareness of Government Legal Requirements & Regulations – In establishing this business my client was relying on me for more than the average business owner to be aware of the requirements and regulations. With international trade we had to liaise with Industry Canada and Canadian Border Services to determine transport of matériel. I had to clarify with MG the tax implications of a Cdn. Corp. as well as his responsibilities as a sole director. We went over the rules of securing money back from the federal SR&ED program. I setup a meeting with a senior member of my advisory board who is an expert in structuring angel investments who gave MG advice prior to closing the deal.

Demonstrates Organizational Skills – In the course of 5 weeks I setup a Canadian corporation, opened a Vancouver office for the corporation, sourced and setup meetings with angel investors, setup multiple conference calls and video conferencing while working full time at SUCCESS. With limited time at my disposal and my client from Winnipeg and Mexico I needed to be very effective with each meeting and efficient.

Managing Information – Since my client was an Engineer and a Project Manager I felt I should help him implement some MIS into his business. MIS is a subset of the overall internal controls of a business covering the application of people, documents, technologies, and procedures by management and I felt my client should start the business off on the right foot. We determined his needs and he set up an excel program that managed costs and allowed him to give his angel investors considerable data in his cost breakdown. We also found considerable information from Industry Canada db's and organized information from numerous government services.

Develop and Maintain Inventory of Resources – As mentioned earlier capacity building and synergy is of paramount importance in my manner of counseling. I have access to 3 levels of government for help for small business. I have strategic alliances with 4 Boards of

Analyze the location for potential problems/opportunities

Discuss issues regarding HR

<u>Process and skills used</u>

<u>Assist Client to Conduct Situational Analysis</u> – The client is a Canadian citizen originally from China who lacks knowledge of Cdn. Culture and business methodology. I worked with CG to determine who her client base was and what the psychographics of this demographic would be. We met in my office and discussed the amount of rent she could afford and made up a profile of a typical client. We assessed locations in terms of distance to her home, finances she had available as well as potential for finding customers. She has school age children so considerations had to be taken to have another employee and one part time person to cover shifts for the retail operation.

The psychographics of values, motivations and goals are the beginning of a directed targeting of potential customers based on the lifestyle patterns of the customer versus functionality driven demographics. I ask my client to answer the following questions and usually other questions will come up as well.

Is there a clustering effect of typical businesses that fit your general principles and lifestyle that may use your services in this market area?

Can you affordably reach them?

Can they afford you the lifestyle you want to live?

Is there a possibility of common networking possibilities?

CG is a very independent woman, community aware and likes to work with other like-minded 'business women'. Item one above was a determining factor in her securing a business close to other businesses owned and operated by women. She opened next to a Midwife clinic and a women's clothing store aptly named Benwick & Woman because she wasn't a man and had a daughter not a son. The block in which her store is located has an abundance of shops who support each other and customers are drawn to them as well for similar reasons.

Assist Client to Assess Client Preparedness –After we had done a situational analysis I met with CG to assess whether she was up for the challenges of the retail operation. She had shown some trepidation at risking her money and the signing of a long term contract was stressful. To her credit she had done extensive market research and had determined that the eastern side of Vancouver provided an opportunity with small businesses nearby and reasonable rents. She had discussed after school care with friends and family with respect to the interlude between when her husband came home from work and when her part time employee would work. She told me the situational analysis we had done the week previous had allayed some fears and she had gone home with a game plan and worked out a lot of our shared concerns.

Assist Client in Identifying Alternatives- I am a firm believer in having backup plans. We looked at various scenarios for her retail store. Location was the biggest challenge but with a small selection available we needed to look at 3 different areas of Vancouver and assess the pros and cons of each. One location had all the amenities, fit her demographics but needed extensive renovations which the landlord would not provide. She felt confident that if the first location failed to materialize she had options.

We went to 2 other locations in different parts of Vancouver to compare prices, demographics and feasibility. She had picked a lovely location on the Westside of Vancouver that was homey, airy and would have provided her a great working environment. The rent was considerably lower than offices only a block away. I pointed out that she should check recent business activity in that spot. What she found was there had been 6 businesses in that space in a span of only 5 years. I had surmised that I knew the reasons but had CG assess the location from her point of view. I asked her to park her car at 9 in the morning out front of the store and count walk by traffic. I also suggested she walk around the neighborhood and see what was happening. The next morning, CG arrived in front of the shop and couldn't park as it was a no parking rush hour street, as well the bus stop out front effectively cut out more parking and the bus shelter hid the signage on the storefront. When CG had taken her walk around the shop she noted that there was only resident parking on every street surrounding the retail block and 2 blocks further down the street on the same side were 3 large graphic/photocopy stores. The space now seemed less than ideal thus reflecting the cheap rent. We moved on to the next location on a **busy** downtown Vancouver Street. The space had a lot going for it too but the price was 5 times higher than the choice she eventually selected. Since her main marketing idea was to bring people into her store with a lost leader inexpensive photocopying service she would never have made the rent in that location.

We needed to assess the driving distances because driving times to and from home was crucial to child care issues. We worked together on finding back-ups for the children in the event an employee called in sick or other problems presented themselves.

Assist Client in Developing an Action Plan – During the Business Plan process a month earlier, CG, had developed an action plan for her business so she was comfortable with the process. We met over coffee to come up with very specific action plan/goals in order for her to secure her retail shop. We worked on a comparative chart for the different locations, which permits, licenses were required, some extra funding issues had to be addressed, procurement of office equipment e.g. photocopiers, etc. and of course a strategy for negotiating the lease. The goals we determined had to coincide with the property lease as some of the goals hinged on the location. Our coffee meeting turned into lunch and I assisted CG to determine her needs and the action plan resulted.

Assist Client in Identifying Time Frames –Once CG had outlined her goals I helped CG put together a realistic time frame that she felt she could accomplish. Obviously the location had to be secured first then everything else would fall in place but I reminded her that once she signed the lease her other actionable goals would have to follow quickly. I reminded her that each passing day without revenue would be to the detriment of the business.

Perform Site Visit Observations– I have performed hundreds of site visits to assess clients working environment, organizational skills, inventory levels, etc, but in CG's case I went with her and her real estate agent to the favored prospective location to conduct an analysis as to the viability of the location. Her favored location was 3 blocks from the primary location in my mind (site B) and was 1/3 of the cost of site B.

I pointed out that usually the reason for a lower rent was reduced customer activity. I wanted her to make a considered decision and pointed out that the parking restrictions were considerable at her site while Site B being across the street had great parking and had no restrictions at evening rush hour. I reminded her that many people favored locations within walking distance of busy stores and amenities, e.g. Starbucks, banks, major chain stores and although her choice was good site B was adjacent to all of those desirable 'draw' stores.

I asked CG to notice that the carpets were well worn and painting and other upgrades would be needed before she could move in. When she asked the leasing agent for relief for these items she was told renovations would have to be at her cost.

When all the factors in the location was weighed she made the decision to lease Site B; the more expensive location but with considerable more traffic and a more favorable landlord.

Assist Client in Identification of Human Resources– My client CG secured her retail shop and then asked for a meeting 2 weeks later to discuss her prospective employees. I met CG at her shop and I asked her what she understood about current employment issues to get a better understanding of where to begin. She was very naïve and although she had been in business in China she did not know about CRA or employment regulations in Vancouver. She told me she had intended to 'hire' a salesperson on 100% commission. I pointed out that she needed to provide a base salary to be in compliance with CRA. She also shyly told me she was paying a friend 'under the table' wages. I gave her some handouts I brought from my office that explained why the 'underground' economy was not good for her business and I explained that she would not be able to get tax benefits if she failed to follow CRA regulations.

<u>Outcomes</u>

Assess her needs for a retail location- CG had several possible locations chosen for her retail store. I helped her make a very solid choice by giving her the pros and cons of each location without the emotional attachment she had for each location.

Develop an action plan – The retail location had numerous things that needed to be done in a sequence once the location was chosen. CG followed a plan to fruition and has made a go of the business. She has been in the location for 1.5 years and while the beginning was rough she is in a positive cash position.

Source and secure a retail location- She found a retail location that met her needs and while higher this price proved to be a more prudent choice in the long term because the customer base was larger.

Help client with HR problems and compliance issues- CG had started to run afoul of convention when she started her business but we quickly set her straight with a bookkeeper (who showed her the tax savings) and secured a better employee by paying a base salary as well as a good percent of sales.

Case Study Number 4

Startup, R&D, Invention Development

Name: Gary C. Bizzo, APEC CBC

Client: Corp (Client- Veronica), limited company

Length of Intervention: 14 hours

Location: Bizzo Management Group, Office and Client's premises, Vancouver

Stage in Business: Startup

Background

My client, Veronica, is a very confident middle aged married woman in Vancouver. She was being mentored by me and would soon be required to implement a comprehensive business plan.

Veronica had been selected to work with because of her idea of a robotic doll that could do sign language for deaf children.

She had several issues with this product. Primarily she did not have an engineering background and would have to rely on professionals to make her invention and her product work. Veronica had spent over $40,000 of her own capital to have a technical designer develop technical drawings of the robot. She also secured a patent in the US and Canada.

Specifics of counseling objectives

Assess the opportunities for the product

Develop an action plan

Assist the client in product R&D

Identify sources of finance

Process and skills used

<u>Assist Client in Identification of Opportunities</u> – The client is a creative individual who has sought business skills in order to put together a product which she thinks will allow children to learn sign language easier and in a fun manner. I wanted Veronica to fully research and identify all the avenues open for her product, the most lucrative segment for revenue ability and the easiest way to get the product to market. We met in my office and discussed the amount of work she had done on the project to date.

We worked over the course of those months in finding the end user with simple market research as well as working with the obvious stakeholders which included the Canadian Association of the Deaf, Center of Abilities and the Greater Vancouver Association of the Deaf.

The problem with her product was immediately identified – price. We worked on finding the target market that could support a high price and bringing this product to market.

I assisted Veronica in developing an action plan that would take her through the steps to analyze costs and time frames so she could up with the money needed to go ahead.

With some directed research we determined that stores could not sell a $400 item. By identifying it as a learning tool it was more appropriate than calling it a mechanical toy or doll.

I assisted Veronica in meeting with the President of Mattel in NYC to determine our feeling that the toy market was not the correct one. She got a lot of help from Mattel in helping us identify that schools for the deaf and facilities funded by government were more likely to purchase a learning aid. I helped Veronica find similar products to provide a business model for her Business Plan and while the theoretical aspects were coming to a head we needed to address the R& D aspects and sources of funding.

<u>Assist Client Product Development</u>–After we had done a situational analysis I met with Veronica to assess whether she was up for the challenges of taking this learning tool to market. I wanted Veronica to fully understand the process of not only taking the

product to market but also to fully realize the large task ahead of her while trying to develop her product from concept through prototyping to salable product.

After we identified the steps required to complete the product from mechanical drawings I assisted her in finding the right people to move from step to step of R&D. Since this product was only, in effect, a technical manual without prototyping I gave her ideas on how to proceed with little capital and the possibility that costs could easily skyrocket if she chose the wrong direction and perhaps the wrong production company.

I helped her analyze and determine that she could produce the prototype as an escalating cost real model at a cost of $80,000 at a minimum or as a virtual modeling project. The latter at a cost of $8000 fit her budget. She was delighted to know that the device would look real, provide her with insights into making changes and fit her action plan which would allow her to show possible investors how the product would look and work without a complete working model.

<u>Identify Sources & types of Financing</u>- I knew we were going to have challenges finding money to develop the product over and above finding the market. Her financial resources were being depleted mainly from early spending that was not targeted to more appropriate avenues.

We determined that although bank financing was an option we would try to set Veronica up with possible investors who had the same vision and could see her potential. She was prepared to give up to 30% of her business to a suitable investor who hopefully would be a working partner.

We sourced out the value of going after SR&ED government money for her sweat and financial investment. I aided her in setting up small equity positions for the virtual modeler, a contract lawyer and found a mentor who would work gratis to guide her through technical areas in which I was not qualified.

She selected the small equity positions and a line of credit to secure a higher position for her when she did find investment capital.

Outcomes

Assess the opportunities for the product – Veronica had several markets and as many strategies to get her robot to market. I helped her make the choice of making it a learning tool and marketing it to the institutional market at a higher profit margin.

Develop an action plan – Veronica's sequence of R&D was job critical and as some overlap was concerned and costs were very high crucial decisions had to be planned ahead.

Assist the client in product R&D – It quickly became clear that she could spend well over $200,000 to get a prototype developed. With some good moves we felt back-end financing could allow her to get away with less of a prototype if she found an investor who could see the big picture from the virtual modeling. The virtual modeling was good enough that you felt you could touch it through the monitor. We also felt an investor might look more favorably on an inventor who understood production costs and took a more prudent development option.

Identify sources of finance- Standard invention wisdom is that you build a product and manufacturer it, license it or sell it. In Veronica's case without a working model her options were very limited. By going after R&D tax breaks, LC's and equity participation the end result was less costly, provided easily made improvements to her robot and actually made the project proceed faster.

Update:

Veronica did produce the Virtual model and we found an agent to represent her to investors. She understood it would be a long process and is happy with the process and progress. An upside is that while she was developing the robot to teach deaf children she came up with the idea of a storybook for children having a cast of children all of whom have 'disabilities'. The catch is that they also each have 1 superpower to compensate. It is being hailed as a tool to teach equality, issues with persons with disabilities and even bullying issues. Several publishers are considering the project.

Case Study Number 5

Growth, Marketing Land Development Corp

Name: Gary C. Bizzo, APEC CBC

Client: Corp (Client- CEO, Marantz), limited company

Length of Intervention: 100 hours

Location: Client's Offices, Vancouver

Stage in Business: Startup

Background

My client, Marantz, is a corporation that was formed in Saskatchewan for the purpose of buying up large tracks of farmland for consolidation. The CEO and President are close friends of mine and contracted me to work with them on this new project to develop a brand and marketing strategy.

These entrepreneurs grew up together in Saskatchewan and have remained close all their lives. The CEO lives in London and left the President and me to develop a plan to market the new company to rural farmers. They started purchasing land with the acquisition of their parent's former homesteads in rural Sask.

To the farmers of Sask. these two men were considered outsiders coming into their land and buying up land. Most were unaware that the men had been born there and were buying up land that their families had once owned but lost over the years.

The challenges were to purchase land without causing a run on property values, developing trust from the locals and coming across as real farmers.

The commitment for the project, funded by the CEO, was for the purchase of approximately 100,000 hectares most of which were in 'parcels' of land called sections at 660 acres each. These sections are so large that addresses don't exist. They are referred to by latitude and longitude and land designators.

<u>Specifics of counseling objectives</u>

Assist client in developing marketing strategies

Interpret market research

Overcome some major problems and Develop trust

Find an innovative marketing strategy

<u>Process and skills used</u>

<u>Assist Client in Marketing Strategies</u> – The client is a well-funded Multinational Corporation. This vast acquisition of land is a pet project of the owner with an initial capital investment of $20M USD. I worked with them to understand the mindset of the people from whom they were buying land.

The President, Bob, has a lifelong background in Sales and his CEO is a venture capitalist by profession. Their first impulse was to move fast and acquire land randomly to avoid 'talk' of city speculators buying land for an undefined purpose. I helped them understand that they would need to attune their focus to that of the locals.

In our discussion, I worked with them to develop a website with a very 'green' environmental look with sustainability and 'stewards of the earth' as the main theme throughout the website. I knew the history of their families already. I had learned through many discussions that both men had felt a strong attachment to the land their family once owned and yearned for the day they could regain their family homesteads.

I asked them questions about their values, what they felt was missing in rural Saskatchewan and what vision they had for the land when they acquired it. They told me they had originally just wanted to acquire the 1200 hectares once owned by their families. However with our general discussions of values etc. they decided to create the 'big picture' which they then implemented.

I pointed out their options for such large tracks of land. They fully embraced only one; to farm the land as a business. We looked at the community's reaction to these guys coming into 'their' community and went over different options on their boardroom white board as well as pros and cons of each option.

It made a lot of sense to these guys once they decided on the farming to create the green image. The green concept also coincided with the Kyoto Protocol and the international forum on climate change so the focus was practical and relevant.

We came to the conclusion that any major change would be met with an unenthusiastic response from the locals. I helped them put themselves in the shoes of the local farmers so they could become more a part of the community.

We wrote in terms of section land identifiers that the locals could relate to and feel more at ease working with Marantz. After meetings with some locals and the principals we developed a form that was a call to action for those farmers who filled it out to sell their land at a premium to Marantz.

Rumors began that the new company was buying land to setup manufacturing plants or worse - mining. I worked with them to purchase state-of-the-art combines and seeders. Then using film and pictures put it out in advertising that indeed they were farmers. Rumors continued when the large combines were being purchased with cash while farmers used mortgages, loans, etc. and would take years to pay for the farming equipment.

<u>Demonstrate Creative Thinking</u>, <u>Demonstrate Problem Solving Approaches</u>, <u>Interpret & Facilitate Market Research</u>, – The situation analysis process took place once per week and there were signs that distrust was not being mitigated. We commenced market research, focus groups and Stats Canada research which we determined provided us with a possible solution.

The normal size of each land transaction was approx. 1 section which is one mile square. I had enrolled Marantz in a new thought process that had them thinking like farmers again and going back to their roots. The market research indicated that empty nest syndrome was a major problem in rural Sask. As farming became more difficult the children of farmers sought to move out of the area to large cities leaving the parents to mind the farm themselves. We were encountering landowner/empty nesters who were near retirement without an exit strategy or any options but to sell the land with no plan after the sale of their land.

I was reminded that the reason Marantz began this project was to buy their old homesteads. We discussed their reasons for being here and came up with an innovative marketing strategy that involved buying an entire farm but deeding back five acres including the farmers home and outbuildings gratis to the farmer. Five immediate results occurred:

The farmer kept his home and legacy.

The farmer had money so he could hobby farm an acre if he wanted but didn't need to. He could retire.

When friends and neighbors saw how it worked they lined up for their own deal

The farmers appeared to still be the stewards of their own land because they hadn't left the property trust ensued.

Large blocks of land were now being accumulated which made farming by Marantz not only easier but more economical.

<u>Diagnose Client's Business Problems</u> In our discussion it came out that if the land corporation was going to an operating farm it needed good management. We discussed numerous scenarios. I helped them identify several options which once again we went to the white board to make a graphic interpretation of a management structure. I reminded them of the primary reason they bought the land, to reclaim the homestead and asked them how that related to

their new plans. The issues at hand were mainly logistical but also functional. Both men lived far from the property, one in London and one in Vancouver. Neither man had the time commitment nor the skills required to manage a multi million dollar farming conglomerate. I pointed out to them that from past experience with them that their little projects usually developed into large corporations and in the past they found executives to run them. When we identified this project in those terms they understood the differences and similarities to past projects.

It became clear that this 'hobby' farm needed major attention of which neither could afford to provide. The easiest solution was to bring in a senior executive from Vancouver to run the project. Two immediate problems were identified. Firstly, the urban exec would not be in his element and secondly, I pointed out that perhaps the community might not accept him. I reminded them that big changes were going to happen to the community, mainly in terms of economic, but somehow the status quo needed to be addressed.

I helped them determine what the level of authority would be and responsibilities were identified and assigned. It became apparent in our discussions that not only a local person was needed to run the project but that even the title would be an important consideration. I gave them options for project leader titles which seemed inconsequential to them but I pointed out that they needed to allay fears, fit in and create a rural feel to the operation.

They settled on the name Director of Farm Operations. In essence the duties would be that of President or very least Sr. VP, but Director of Farm Operations seemed to be more apropos. Once they felt comfortable with the chain of command, the ideal Director of Farm Operations was clear. He was a very well respected farmer who was among the first to sell his land to the corporation. He was offered the position the next day and immediately accepted.

Outcomes

Assist client in developing marketing strategies- Marantz developed a marketing strategy that actually changed the way people

213

do business in rural Sask. and engaged the farmers as stakeholders in the process.

Interpret market research – The Company had to interpret the common empty nester phenomenon but put a twist on it for family run businesses.

Develop trust – Marantz used extensive references in their marketing referencing language common to those to whom they were marketing. The 'too good to be true' altruism of giving back the homestead to the farmer clinched the trust of the community. Developing new infrastructures for the entire community solidified the trust. A farmer turned Director of Farm Operations tied all the loose ends together.

Find an innovative marketing strategy- By helping my clients think like their customers we developed an innovative marketing strategy that changed the way land is accumulated in Saskatchewan.

Several weeks after the launch of the company and well into 20,000+ hectares purchased, the CEO, told me by telephone that our marketing strategies had changed his thinking. Apparently he did have ulterior motives, in that he wasn't planning to do much farming. Instead he was going to build a biogas plant.

His change in focus had the company hire a full time Farm Manager who has turned the business into a true agricultural corporation. Their choice of the Director of Farm Operations was a good one. The man was born and raised in the area, innovative, well respected and although a quiet man has a great deal of respect in the community. He is a natural leader and has increased revenues beyond the corporation's expectations.

Currently they built what is called a bin farm meaning they have huge storage facilities for grain storage. They have built an infrastructure for local farmers who still own their land so they can share these bins as well. Marantz does the sale of all the grain for everyone. It has turned into a community that is less affected by the poor economy. They now have 50 bins holding 150,000 bushels of grain each. Year two will see a further purchase of 50,000 more acres.

Case Study Number 6

Startup, B2B, Food & Beverage

Name: Gary C. Bizzo, APEC CBC

Client: Corp (Client- Harundi), limited company

Length of Intervention: 35 hours

Location: Bizzo Management Group, Office, Vancouver

Stage in Business: Startup

Background

My client, Harundi, formed a corporation within days of arriving in Canada. He was a recent immigrant to Canada who brought with him an exceptional work ethic and energy.

Harundi' business is to place vending machines in offices in Metro Vancouver for free and service them. He makes his money from sales of the coffee and/or confectionery in the machines.

This 40 year old man from Mumbai has had several businesses in his life with little success. He joined my Self Employment (SEP) program in an effort to break the cycle and to find the correct methods in operating a service-based business.

The SEP provides extensive workshops on each facet of the business plan and more on operations, soft skills development and regulations as well as standard operating procedures in doing a startup. The workshops follow a well defined curriculum which I have developed over several years based on my experience as an entrepreneur.

Harundi, being new to Canada, had his own preconceptions of how to operate a business but didn't know much about Canadian customs and regulations. He had run businesses in the past and had his own conceptions on how to run them. The fact that they were not successful, in his mind, did not reflect on his shortcomings.

My goal was to counsel Harundi on the value and absolute necessity of business planning and to counsel him one to one.

<u>Specifics of counseling objectives</u>

Assist client in understanding the value of business planning

Show the client how planning can be attained with specific tools

Help him understand the planning process by giving him learning options

<u>Process and skills used</u>

<u>Explain Value of Business Planning</u>. I went through the process with Harundi as to why he felt his previous businesses had failed in India. I pointed out that he had opened the doors to a business without understanding the concept of location intelligence, demographics and had no systems in place. He had typically received deals on products that he would then sell to the public, however, he had no idea if the products were wanted or needed, yet he did have them for sale with the old feeling 'if I open my doors they will come'.

In our discussions I pointed out that perhaps if he had planned his company in advance in terms of sales strategies, location management and fiscal policy things might have turned out differently.

We began with the vision of his business and how he wanted to visualize the new company. His mission statement seemed to empower him once I explained how to define it. Planning his marketing and sales campaign and strategies were eye-openers to Harundi as I explained the psychological basis for marketing to customers. He understood immediately and we worked on helping him visualize and effective marketing campaign in his style. Harundi needed considerable help in understanding the financial analysis in business planning but funny enough took easily when showed spreadsheets via Excel.

I helped him face the challenges of planning for the future and once the process was explained to him I helped him coordinate an effective business plan.

<u>Assess Client's Legal & Credit Status</u> – During the planning process we discussed the various business structures open to Harundi. He originally had planned to operate the business as a sole proprietor as he had done in the past in India. We discussed liability issues and I pointed out the issues he may face if there were any problems with his vending machines in his customers places of work. His products included food, hot drinks, large machines that could tumble on an unsuspecting employee, etc. I explained other structures including incorporation that would protect him from liability.

I wanted Harundi to consider down the road when he needed to hire employees to manage his vending machines. I asked him to consider if an employee had "an accident" at his customer's place of work injured him and harmed a delicate piece of equipment at his customer's place of business. I pointed out that as a sole proprietor if he was slapped with a lawsuit, he could lose all his assets, savings, house, and marriage. If Harundi had his company incorporated, his business and personal life would have been separated and had an additional layer of protection. Incorporation reduces disasters.

With several options in mind for his business structure including a possible partnership with an investor down the road he decided on incorporating. I worked with Harundi to help him understand the tax and credit implications of incorporation and how new business owners separate personal and business credit histories and establish separate business credit. He didn't require financing but I suggested that a business credit card would be useful for his purchases and how the corporation was treated by the law as a separate entity. While Harundi's personal credit has a high FICO score I helped him understand that the corporation need its own credit and that most banks would probably require him to have a personal guarantee associated with any loans, leases or transaction requiring credit.

Introduce Client to Business Planning Tools - We conducted an analysis, in point form, based on the various sections comprising a typical business plan. Harundi had been very confident while we were going over the business planning process but I felt that once he was left to his own devices he would be overwhelmed. He is very independent and likes to move ahead quickly and up to now with little thought for planning. I pointed out that once he understood the processes involved in the planning of his new company the next step was to write the plan.

We both worked on a SWOT analysis, situational analysis and I showed him how he could accomplish complex market research on his own. I often use a template for a business plan and helped him understand the different sections by making notes in the margins in plain English so he could relate to the plan as he filled in the sections. When we developed the competition matrix again he had a eureka moment. He understood the strategies when numbers were placed side by side and benefits lined up next to each other

Identify Learning Opportunities - In our discussion it came out that although Harundi is an intelligent man, listening to workshops and taking notes was not an effective learning tool for him. Harundi reacted much better to visuals so we found YouTube videos, as well as my Library materials that illustrated different points and strategies needed in the development of a business plan. We utilized white boards where applicable to draw flowcharts and make point form analysis for Harundi to understand

I also suggested that we visit a few successful businesses and we did a 'road trip' visiting some existing clients' operations that were doing very well. In each location over the course of the day Harundi saw first hand how others accomplished tasks that he needed to master as well.

Accounting and bookkeeping were initial problems for Harundi. I set him up with a financial mentor who helped him setup a chart of accounts and identified after discussion typical expenses that he could incorporate into a spreadsheet.

Outcomes

Explaining the value of the Business planning process- Harundi learned that planning was not only a good prerequisite for an effective successful Business but that is was a necessary way to focus on issues facing the business on a day to day as well as in the long term basis.

Legal and credit status- Harundi had always operated as sole proprietor and after being aware of corporations felt liability and tax benefits fit more into his future goals.

Introduce Client to Business Planning Tools –With an action plan in hand and a competition matrix he was able to plan for the year while identifying his competitive advantage over his competition. We used a template for the plan which gave him hints at what to place in the sections.

Learning Opportunities - Harundi found it much easier to develop his business plan once we helped him identify what learning method worked better for him. He is more of a visual person so by coupling videos with white board presentations he developed a Business plan that is still guiding his business 4 years later. The road trip concept really allowed Harundi to see the plan in action. He took bits of several businesses to create his own systems.

Case Study Number 7

Growth, Service Industry

Name: Gary C. Bizzo, APEC CBC

Client: Corp (Client-'Ernesto'),

Length of Intervention: 98 hours

Location: Bizzo Management Group, office/client's home, Vancouver

Stage in Business: Startup

Background

 My client, Ernesto, formed a corporation a year before my involvement with him as a counselor. He was an immigrant to Canada from Honduras who brought with him an exceptional work ethic, energy and his immediate family including mother.

 Ernesto had been working for the top 3 commercial cleaning businesses since arriving in Canada 4 years ago. Ernesto's resume indicates that he was self employed in retail in his home country.

 This 39 year old man has seen some success before I took him on as a client. Although he had received extensive training and time spent with our coaching staff there always seemed to be a challenge taking his business to the next level.

 I felt it was important to meet him in his own surroundings, being his home, so that we could break down any barriers and make him more open and comfortable talking to me. I brought the coffees and we made appointments at his home when his siblings and mother were not at home giving us privacy.

 Ernesto has a pleasing personality and comes across as a very quiet, shy man. I had a feeling that the exterior was based on a lack of confidence with the English language and cultural differences

My goal was to counsel Ernesto one to one, find the barriers to his success and offer strategies to grow his business.

Specifics of counseling objectives

Assist client in developing a SWOT analysis,

Work on a marketing strategy, inc. identifying customer bases

Help him understand the planning process by giving him learning options

Process and skills used

Conduct Situational Analysis; Conduct Market Analysis. I explained the internal versus external aspects of a situational analysis, commonly referred to as a SWOT analysis. It's great how the acronym can stick in the client's mind for future analysis.

Strengths – The Client is a dedicated, reliable person who is committed to providing an exceptional cleaning service to his customers. He employs like minded persons including his mother who works diligently and are equally as reliable on the job.

Ernesto also had sufficient capital from savings to keep the business afloat while waiting for clients to pay. He has extensive experience working for the top janitorial companies in Vancouver. He knows his operational side of the business.

Weaknesses – After numerous hours of discussions it became clear the type of business Ernesto chose and the English language defined his business structure. He started the cleaning business based on experience of course, but mainly because he could work alone at night without interaction with the average Canadian due to what he perceived as his language issues. Ernesto operates at a very high language level and is well past the typical Grade 12 English equivalent that I normally see in business.

Ernesto's other weakness still hinged on his English but was easier to change. Although he is a citizen his English made him feel inferior to other Canadians. Because of the inferiority, he is not able to instigate a conversation, sales call, or phone call to those in a power position particularly if it's a future client situation. He has found another way of securing business. He buys existing contracts from other janitorial businesses and not only pays them a high value for the contract but also pays a percentage of the contract each month. From a financial situation, a disaster, but it did solve his immediate problem of how to deal with customers and gave him cash flow.

By talking frankly and setting up goals we developed a scenario which would mitigate his fears. He needed to know he had backup and a team behind him. I tell my clients if they have weaknesses mitigate it by filling the gap from an external source. In Ernesto's strategy we interviewed sales professionals resulting in one I am associated with. We setup a mutually agreeable sales plan with goals and observable milestones. By hiring a sales professional our next plan was to stop the practice of 'buying' contracts.

It became clear that while Ernesto had a good operational knowledge his marketing experience and goal setting skills were failing him.

The sales person would provide telemarketing on a contract basis. They will be responsible for looking for clients and acquiring leads. As the company grows we will be putting in place a telemarketing team that will focus not only on finding new clients but also communicating various others services to customers.

Opportunities – We also worked together to create a unique selling point (USP) that would be his and allow us to differentiate him in the crowded field of professional janitorial companies and a considerable number of home based businesses. That USP was simple, we secured a source of quality Eco-friendly products and marketed the Eco concept to doctors and dentist offices which had a different set of needs as opposed to a regular office.

The focus on environmentally friendly products is a constant theme among Vancouverites and whether they are or not, clients feel it is important as an image to appear to so.

<u>Threat</u> -

One of the potential threats is the decreasing of the construction boom and the slowdown of possible business after the Olympics. Our strategy will be to exceed customer expectations to establish great relationships to maintain our client base even after the 2010 Olympics. Larger companies may see the environmentally – friendly services as a niche as well but as first adopters Ernesto will make a reputation as the first to provide this service with little or no increase in pricing.

<u>Conduct Financial Analysis</u> - We conducted an analysis in point form based on the line items on his 3 year proforma. Ernesto had plans to take his business to the next step by securing a Canadian Youth Business Foundation loan for $30k. He needed simple but accurate financials for the bank.

Ernesto's financials indicated that because of the influx of cash coming in every month from the contracts the situation looked better than it was in reality. He was liquid at the first of the month but when he had to pay his bills his costs showed a different story.

His accounts receivable edged up to 45 days and he was carrying his 4 employees from one month to the next. With his credit rating being good with a FICO over 920 he would be able to leverage his volume to borrow money. In his case it was a case of expanding or quitting. Financially there was little else to do.

Ernesto's profitability would dramatically increase if he could get rid of subcontracted accounts that he had bought by replacing them with non-subcontracted accounts that the sale person would pickup. The difference added more than 30% to his bottom line.

<u>Analyze Organizational Behavior: Identify Personality Types</u> - In all of our discussions it came out that although Ernesto is an intelligent man, he knew that his limitations needed to be mitigated and was prepared to do so at the earliest opportunity. Ernesto constantly practiced his assertiveness on me which was a bit

humorous but gave us opportunities to address which techniques were working and which would not work for Ernesto.

He is a compassionate man who had put in his business plan that he wanted to be an employer who listened to his workers, treated them with respect and paid them above average wages.

His role as the Operations Manager was perfect for his desired and perceived role in the operation. He did not want to sell and frankly he was not good at it. We identified areas he could improve his organizational abilities in terms of scheduling, geographic areas he could market to in order to have a group of businesses that his employees could easily move through each evening. Most contracts took less than 3 hours so he would need to keep his employees busy working versus traveling.

We realized Ernesto's mother in the business was a powerful figure and worthy of listening. She was good as a supervisor as one would suspect, wanting to take care of her son's business affairs. She also held to the same principles Ernesto did about employees. I think placing her in a supervisory position added a valuable buffer between the staff and the boss. His employees were selected for their ability to work unsupervised on occasion and diligence.

Our role from the beginning was to have Ernesto work ON the business not IN it so the addition of the sales person while on contract as a test position would prove the value of having someone else create contracts. I suggested that the two of us interview possible telemarketers and sales persons. After the first two, Ernesto took a more active role in choosing someone not only qualified but who had a temperament that matched his easy going management style. Thankfully, Ernesto selected a colleague of mine who I also felt was a good match with him and someone who would complement him in making good sales and marketing decisions. Of course, Bookkeeping and accounting were outsourced so that the operations side was very easily defined and allowed for Ernesto to 'own' the role. We set him up with a financial mentor to help him monitor his accounts and help him with his planning.

Outcomes

Doing a SWOT and market analysis opened Ernesto's eyes and gave him the tools to move ahead past the confidence issues he faced. SWOT also allowed him the vision to open himself up to working with advisors and mentors.

I helped him to redefine a typical janitorial business which focuses on a market niche providing environmentally friendly cleaning products which are comparable in price but exhibit better cleaning results than the highly potent chemicals other janitorial companies use. With an action plan in hand and a competition matrix he was able to plan for the year while identifying his competitive advantage over his competition.

Organizational analysis and identifying personality types- Ernesto is a complex man with clear issues that he is addressing. The goal was to take him out of the equation by replacing critical areas with professionals which in the long term would make him more money.

With his challenges addressed and changes made, Ernesto redeveloped his business plan including new financials which gave the bank a much more favorable financial ratio to base a loan on. Ernesto secured two loans each for $15,000 from the CYBF and BDC. A side benefit to the loans is that they come with a mentor who is assigned to watch the growth of his business.

Case Study Number 8

Startup, Distribution Hospitality

Name: Gary C. Bizzo, APEC CBC

Client: Corp (Client-'Danika'),

Length of Intervention: 30 hours

Location: SUCCESS office, Vancouver

Stage in Business: Startup

Background

My client, Danika, was a client with a Self Employment Program at SUCCESS Business & Economic Development Center. She had formed a corporation after the first week of my involvement with her as a counselor. Her business is to supply plastic packages of ice in cubes to bars, restaurants and catering companies. These 'ice cubes' are easily identifiable and easily differentiated from her competition by cube size and bag size.

She is energetic, has a strong focus and has a competent partner to help and support her.

Danika had been working with her father as he attempted to start an ice manufacturing business in Whistler, BC. After several months of planning they felt a manufacturing plant was not feasible. Danika took her father's plan and modified it to suit a distribution company instead. Danika's resume indicates that she was self employed in retail in the past.

This 32 year old woman has a partner who will share operational duties, support from her family but requires a loan from the Canadian Youth Business Foundation. Luckily I am the Chairman of the Loan Committee. My staff will assess her business plan and her abilities and I will myself from the decision making process. The fact that she has presented her plan already to our Advisory Board is considered by the CYBF as an important process to a positive outcome.

I felt it was important to meet in my offices which I do with any female client to avoid any possible innuendos or miscommunication.

My goal was to counsel Danika one to one, find the barriers to her success and offer strategies to grow her business. I had to take into account her partner's involvement and sought to include her when possible in coaching at Danika's direction.

Specifics of counseling objectives

Incorporate her business

Assist client in determining best possible source of material (ice)

Work on helping her assess her credit needs and help her create a good financial plan

Help her understand her role and that of her partner so that a partnership agreement can be in place before the loan was approved.

Help her maintain her role as the management/leadership role while her partner assumed a sales function

I would be helping her with a Financial Analysis

Process and skills used

Recognize Need for Record Keeping/ Accounting Systems- Danika indicated she wanted to incorporate as soon as we met for counseling. She was concerned about liabilities and she had a business partner. I helped her realize that she needed to understand not only the legal aspects of the incorporation but needed to fully understand the need for accurate records and accounting systems for the purposes of a loan, HST payments and corporate taxes at the end of her fiscal year. She also needed accurate records for her partner to be satisfied as Danika would be running the management of the operation.

We identified QuickBooks as the method of record keeping and with that purchased, I suggested she opt for the companion Quick tax for corporations. Although many professional financial people use Simply Accounting, we've experimented with both over the years and have found QuickBooks to be more user friendly for the average client. Since she had skill on QuickBooks this was a good match.

Access & Apply Statistical Data, Interpret Credit Procedures, Assist Client in Financial Analysis. I explained to Danika the data she needed to collect in order to make a calculated and detailed analysis of her product costing and viability of each supplier she had previously identified.

Danika had previously assumed that her father's business, although robust and analyzed, may not have been too far off the track. I pointed out that they had done a fairly detailed business plan and perhaps their first analysis may not have been too far off in their determination that distribution would garner more revenue than a full blown manufacturing plant.

I set her up with an analyst at the BC Small Business Center in downtown Vancouver to access statistical data from their records as far as local labor market information pertaining to manufacturing and distribution channels. I wanted her to see for herself that the competition was well entrenched and to realize that her father's evaluation was correct. I wanted Danika to find out the competition, how long they have been in the local market, the size of the businesses, were they locally based or part of a larger organization? I wanted her to analyze whether she could purchase product from outside the local market, costs of delivery including brokerage fees, transportation and storage costs

The research I helped her with indicated that the local market was so well entrenched in both fields that price and some differentiation would be the only way to acquire market share. Both could be attained by a US manufacturer keen to enter the CDN market.

We came up with a solution to import prepackaged ice with her brand, "On the Rocks" on the bags of a different size than her local competition. The challenges were to compare pricing models for US versus CDN pricing (as it turned out with the rising CDN dollar it was the best choice), brokerage fees and duty if any.

The purchase of US based product of that with a very short life span (ice) required a great deal of cost analysis, comparative analysis to local and sufficient backup and operational resources to maintain her sustainability.

We determined that the CYBF loan would work at $15k if she obtained the matching BDC loan of $15k. This provided her cash flow with low interest and no payments on the principal for the first year (CYBF portion only). This allowed her to purchase a refrigerated 5 ton van and gave her a buffer for 6 months. We had a discussion around security, personal guarantees and what could happen if the loan were realized. She felt confident she could manage the interest only aspect of the loan in the first year until they were established.

As for the financing I pointed out the liabilities to her and Danika's partner, the need for a tight partnership agreement and the effect of interest and no principal on the length of the loan she was seeking. I went over the Equifax report with her and identified some things that needed explanation when she applied for the loans. I helped her determine that she needed her partner to be equally responsible and that she needed to provide a report as well.

By talking frankly and setting up goals we developed a scenario which would mitigate financial fears because of ignorance, liability issues and systems to make sure cash flow was used effectively once acquired. Her credit was quite good and the family had offered to step-up in the event a loan was not accessed.

I helped Danika assess the viability, stability and profitability of her business. We went over her income statement, balance sheet and Statement of Cash Flows. I helped her understand how her statement of Cash Flow showed her what would affect cash such as depreciation, accounts receivable and accounts payable.

Danika understands the costs of goods very well and knew her projections had to be very accurate. We compared her liquidity analysis ratios, current and quick ratios and they were within expected norms. Her only major asset being the 5 ton truck made analysis fairly simple. The operation is fairly small at present so projections were easily attained. Her forecasting had expected highs and lows based on traditional and usual seasonal trends.

Access Client's Management Abilities, Assess Client's Leadership Skills

Danika was assumed to be the person with the role of management in the partnership.

I met with Danika and her partner and had each write the job description of the other. Danika's partner, Amanda, was clearly the sales person throughout the meeting with some great points on sales techniques and marketing strategies. However, Danika effectively kept the meeting on focus and was clearly in charge of the business.

Danika is a firm believer in the EMyth theory of management as espoused by one of my partners, Michael E. Gerber. I have pointed out to her the efficacies of the technician becoming the manager then becoming the entrepreneur and she took to that concept very well.

The great part of this is that she leads the business with considered effectiveness and effectively dispels the myth that all managers are not leaders. She is effective and people take notice.

Demonstrate Professionalism - In all of our discussions I was aware of my status as not only her counselor but the Manager of a program which support her financially throughout the process of setting up her business. I needed to be aware of the possible fallout of an inappropriate comment, an inappropriate meeting place as well as making sure Danika's partner, who was not my client, was adequately protected and informed of major developments.

In terms of her loan application, I had recused myself from approving her loan and had set up others in my office to adequately analyze and assess her loan application.

<u>Outcomes</u>

Danika incorporated her business with 2 shareholders and setup accounting and tax systems to be able to maintain records for audit, partnership and loan purposes.

Danika had identified the correct product, in terms of price/quality, to purchase, having also used her research to identify that distribution was the key to her success not manufacturing. This in itself was the single most effective choice she made to have a successful outcome.

With the data and further research she was able to find ways to reduce taxes and her product did not have duty attached from the USA

We assessed her credit worthiness, explained the value of all parties (partner) being involved the transparent loan application process

With her exceptional business plan and support she obtained a $15k CYBF loan and a matching loan from BDC. While the interest is only required on the first loan during the first year, the latter requires payments of principal and interest so as not to have an adverse effect in year 2 where both loans coming in at full payback might be very high.

Her leadership and management skills were well suited to her relationship with her partner as well as her suppliers.

I demonstrated professional and ethical conduct in keeping with APEC Biz guidelines

Case Study Number 9

Startup, Health Industry

Name: Gary C. Bizzo, APEC CBC

Client: Sole Proprietor (Client-'Arima'),

Length of Intervention: 1 hour

Location: Bizzo Management Group office, Vancouver

Stage in Business: Startup

Background

    My client, Arima, is an Iraqi woman of Muslim faith. Her faith is a crucial component as to how I worked with her during a one hour interview to determine her personal and business viability and acceptance as a client in Vancouver.

    I had seen her when she made an appointment for an interview. She came well prepared for an assessment interview for a place in the next intake of entrepreneurs at our centre.

    Her business idea was that of a Doula, a person who supports a woman through pregnancy and works with the patient and a midwife or doctor.

    In Iraq she was a qualified midwife with credentials. In Canada she needed to downgrade her credentials and under Canadian regulations could only work as a Doula rather than the more qualified Midwife.

    Arima wore the traditional clothing associated with woman of the Muslim faith. A head garment, a Hijab, and loose clothing covered her body. I felt she was a very religious Iraqi.

    My goal was to counsel and to interview Arima, one to one, find the barriers to her success starting a business in Canada, determine if we could help her setup a business utilizing her strengths and offer strategies to grow her business. I had to take into account her business idea, her ability to adapt to Canadian customs, her entrepreneurial level, interpersonal skills and her religion in order to deal with her effectively as a counselor.

Specifics of counseling objectives

Assess her business in terms of acceptability to our program and the validity of the business.

Assess her in relation to her personal skills and other personal skills needed to enter a self employment program and to enter the business community in Canada

Process and skills used

Identify with Sensitive Issues – I understood that Amira was a woman of Muslim faith and decided beforehand (when I saw her in our lobby prior to the meeting) to determine her customs. I found that she cannot 'shake hands' with a man other than her husband and to do so would be a problem. It was also not appropriate for her to meet a man alone.

I decided to avoid the problem by not offering my hand as I normally would and ask my assistant (a woman) to offer her hand in a token of introduction. I always conduct interviews with my assistant to avoid any problems in the future due to misunderstandings and also to clarify any points of contention.

I welcomed Amira to our office and introduced her to my assistant at which time they shook hands. Our conflict was averted. It is common for us to assess clients before a meeting to make sure we do make adjustments to their customs.

Demonstrate Confidentiality- Arima indicated she was new to Canada and did not have a great deal of trust of business persons. She felt that her idea of a Doula with her religious background required a higher degree of confidentiality because she wanted to choose an area that had one other practitioner in her field and didn't want that person to find out she was setting up a business to compete.

I produced a Non disclosure agreement which my assistant and I signed and gave Arima the original with a copy attached to her business application. This is standard procedure.

<u>Apply Interview Techniques, Assess Interpersonal Skills</u> – I felt it was important to evaluate her soft skills since being a Doula required intensive interpersonal skills and empathy. She had excellent verbal skills which I found out by using open-ended questions. Although she had a strong accent her English was exceptional having gone to American University in Iraq.

I had already determined her writing skills when I perused her application to my program. Her answers were clear, well written and indicated she had taken considerable time to complete the 19 pages application.

I asked Amira about her strengths and weaknesses which gave me a good indication of her integrity and honesty. I used a questioning & listening strategy including: probing open ended questions to discover in what situation she might 'close down'. From that I drilled down and explored how she could mitigate her identified weaknesses. I got Arima's agreement for an action plan/follow up so that she could incorporate them into a SWOT analysis. She was very open and was very self effacing in her answers.

I felt it was important to assess Arima's interpersonal skills and whether she was able and willing to be part of the dynamics of an intake of instruction which had 12 other participants. They would be sharing information for several weeks full time and it was important that she be an active participant for group dynamics to be positive and uplifting.

I assessed her resume for past examples of teamwork and organizations she had belonged to and asked her about her coworkers in previous jobs. I asked if she had conflicts in the past and how she had dealt with them.

I was quite happy with the results as I only had one hour to perform all the goals I had set out to work on with Arima.

Interpret and Apply Verbal Communications When interviewing Arima it was important to listen carefully as she had a thick accent. I felt it was important to be able to be very clear in my conversation with her to make her comfortable and to get the information I needed to make a clear determination of how to help her and to determine if she would be viable for my program.

We engaged in a conversation about her family and how she felt about being in Canada, how she missed home and friends. This basic conversation allowed her to relax. I could tell in her physical demeanor that she was relaxing.

I felt it was important to observe physical cues with Arima. She had sat down with hands at her sides, shyly looking up with head bowed when answering questions. After 10 minutes of conversation she was using hand gestures, was sitting fully upright and was expressing feelings in addition to the facts requested.

By expressing acceptance and understanding without interrupting Arima became more open about her life.

I found out that she was depressed that she couldn't find employment in Canada in her profession. She was worried that if she began her own business that Canadians would not use her service because of her background and would not accept her.

Outcomes

Clearly, the first thing I had to do was to assess her in terms of her ethnicity and make her comfortable in an interview. This was accomplished by some research on cultural differences.

We dealt with issue of confidentiality with a standard non disclosure agreement which also made her more relaxed in the interview

The interview was successful in terms of making the client comfortable and obtaining information needed to make a valid determination of her acceptability to our program.

Through positive interview techniques and her answers I was able to offer her a position in my program. She is now practicing as a Doula specializing in woman of her culture.

Case Study Number 10

Growth, Service Industry

Name: Gary C. Bizzo, APEC CBC

Client: Corp (Client-'Thomas'),

Length of Intervention: 110 hours

Location: Bizzo Management Group office, Vancouver; Carlsbad, California; Telephone, Skype

Stage in Business: Startup (2nd year in Business)

Background

My client, Thomas, is a client I met while on a Training Workshop in California. Thomas is a young man in his 30's who owns a corporation in Toronto with annual sales of approx. $2.5 million. His business is disaster recovery services specializing in mold removal and remediation. He is very passionate about mold having gone through a health crisis some years ago which gave him the impetus to enter the market.

He is a dynamic, type A, determined man and is the sole owner of his business.

Thomas had an 'awakening' while taking a workshop with me in California, being conducted by Michael E. Gerber, famous business coach and author of the EMyth.

With a purpose in mind and focused on expansion, Thomas asked me to help him expand his operation into British Columbia. I entered into a monthly paid relationship with him to counsel him on ways to handle the expansion. This expanded into helping him work on his business at Head office in Toronto as well.

From the outset Thomas indicated he was a type 'A' personality who was an entrepreneur. He runs his business as he sees it and many recommendations typically fall on deaf ears according to a senior manager who commented that Thomas is a micro manager.

Thomas required meetings by telephone, email as well as an occasional trip to Vancouver where we would meet in my home office or my partner's downtown office.

My goal was to counsel Thomas one to one, to offer strategies to grow his business in the BC market and to give him management support as needed while he undertook the expansion. It was important for me to understand the BC market on a provincial level as well as franchise knowledge pertaining to developing and implementation. It was very important that our relationship be based on trust, knowledge and clearly defined in expectations and outcomes.

Considering Thomas had $2.5M in sales in 2010, he only took a $58k salary and had a net profit of $167k which he spent on assets. I assumed there would be some financial counseling as a part of the counseling sessions with him.

Specifics of counseling objectives

Offer guidance on the expansion of a business to another location in the country.

Help Thomas increase his bottom line generally

Work with his new Director of Marketing on developing strategies

Find a method to provide financial accountability

Develop policies, manuals and procedures for the business

Process and skills used

Demonstrate Positive Attitudes- Thomas is a very powerful man who tends to be obsessive about controlling his business and his life. He surrounds himself with people he has known for years; having these people fill roles in his company rather than finding more qualified people outside. I had to project not only good business acumen but a 'can do' attitude that was required for our relationship to grow and flourish.

Frankly, the development of a franchise plan for the province seemed very daunting to me at the beginning of our relationship. I had to constantly focus on what I was thinking before I made comments knowing that any mistakes on my part would be negatively perceived by Thomas. I also knew that Thomas had spent considerable money, time and resources to get to this point. He had many thoughts expressing doubt and concern that would come to the surface in counseling sessions. It was necessary for me to keep a positive outlook which gave him confidence not only in me but in his decisions.

In my observations at the workshop in California when I met Thomas, there were exercises we did over 3 days that gave me an insight into his way of thinking. On one such day he expressed to the facilitator his vision for the company which not only inspired the participants but made Thomas leave the room in tears. The feelings he expressed from putting his aspirations, goals and fears for the future into words was overwhelming. Knowing his reactions in a workshop environment gave me some insight into how to motivate him when he needed it and gave me insight into what type of learner he was and the coaching approach I would later utilize to work with him as a client.

I asked Thomas to develop and write out the vision for his 'new' company. Without the rousing workshop setting he put more clarity into his vision without the feelings 'from being in the moment'. The resulting positive affirmation alleviated his negativity and made my dealings with him easier.

I gave Thomas samples of my work, testimonials from past clients and an action plan which we would follow in terms of direction and timing guidelines.

Apply Discovery Learning Methods, Employ Coaching Techniques- When I compare Thomas thinking and learning processes to the Felder/Silverman model from the 1980's it was easy to determine that Thomas is a sensory learner who prefers concrete, practical, and procedural information. He looks for the facts rather than the intuitive thinker. Thomas is also very much a verbal learner as well. He prefers to hear or read information. Thomas looks for explanations with words. I usually work better with a visual learner. Thomas is a great model for the neural sciences particularly NLP. As mentioned Thomas is a complex man with simplistic, meat and potatoes learning preference to learning.

Thomas is a reflective learner preferring to learn by analysis and loves to work out problems on his own. I think there is a part of him that wants to be the team player and have support from groups to work out some of the tougher problems (Active Learner).

Thomas also falls into the Sequential model of learning. He prefers to have information presented linearly and in an orderly manner. He puts together the details in order to understand the big picture as it emerges. This is more balanced than the other modes as he also has attributes of a global learner where he likes to have some information presented linearly and in an orderly manner.

My goal in our counseling Thomas as to help him tap into the areas on both sides of the continuum and help him think a little more outside the box. Thomas is a man who listens very well, like a sponge, he told me. I felt if I can give him practical, concrete information and procedures I can guide him to the intuitive side by explain how the two may balance and give him a better understanding of what he wants to do with the business. He already showed signs of that when he had his emotional reaction to his vision while we were in California. The understanding that he is sensory, verbal, reflective indicated to me he was a man who wanted and needed a strong plan for the future with no loose ends. He agreed with my perception that he was, as he put it, "the engineer type" of guy, very analytical. I pointed out to him by understanding each aspect of how he learns we could help him be well rounded in both his business and his dealings with customers and employees.

Thomas as very open to change, he sees himself at 32 a man with the world opening to him. We worked on providing balance by understanding the following:

Sensory – Intuitive: Provide both hard facts and general concepts.

Visual – Verbal: Incorporate both visual and verbal cues.

Active – Reflective: Allow both experiential learning and time for evaluation and analysis.

Sequential – Global: Provide detail in a structured way, as well as the big picture.

I pointed out to Thomas that by understanding learning styles he could adapt and expand on how he learns. Since part of his job is training he understood that the people he trained would learn more than just procedures on mold removal from him.

Since most coaching skills rely on the client's skills and their will to accomplish their goals, I had an easy client to work with in Thomas He is one of the most motivated individuals to come along to me in some time. His goals are based on family, health and helping others, the latter being altruistic but very high on his priorities.

Thomas' 'sponge' mentality and analytic skills gave him the tools to see when other soft tools were added to his repertoire. He quickly adapted to the new skills and changes were small but observable. He treated his new found learning skills as tools he could use once he mastered them.

On a high/low matrix coaching model, Thomas is the highly skilled, high willed person. He is a typically high performer and has high goals that are in his case attainable. Thomas works well under the delegate model- give additional goals, praise and endorse and collaborate on decisions.

<u>Develop a Network of Information & Brokering Skills,</u> <u>Assess Financial & Human Resources</u>, <u>Diagnose Emerging Opportunities & Potential Problems</u> When Thomas introduced me to his new Director Marketing I was surprised with his appointment. Charles had experience as a junior marketing executive but was not really qualified

to run a large organization's marketing department. I offered Thomas and Charles advice as part of my agreement on any marketing issues they may require. I also explained the need for HRM policies. I rationalized the discussion by using the expansion and the need of HRM for BC as a way to discuss the issue of the lack of policies in head office.

I explained that HRM techniques would force Thomas and his managers to express their goals with specificity so that they could be understood and undertaken by the workforce, as well as providing the resources needed for them to successfully accomplish their assignments. We discussed, how, HRM techniques, when properly practiced, are expressive of the goals and operating practices of the enterprise overall. HRM is also seen by many to have a key role in risk reduction.

I helped him realize that a dedicated HR person would give him better employees, manage benefits and manage other personnel aspects of the operation. I told him he needed to think of his employees as assets. Quality assets would benefit his organization in ways he hadn't anticipated besides acting as buffer between his family and friends and employment. Thomas is very altruistic but based on his bottom line he understood that an HR policy and plan would make things much smoother both at Toronto and in BC.

I helped Thomas set up an action plan, including a search for someone to actually perform the hiring process for a qualified HR person to work for Thomas With the benefits of performance, evident in improved employee commitment, lower levels of absenteeism and turnover, higher levels of skills and therefore higher productivity, enhanced quality and efficiency would be a welcome result.

With an HR person eventually hired a HRM policy manual was developed.

Thomas required considerable specific expertise primarily in the areas of franchise development in BC and systems analysis in Toronto. I am associated with the Canadian Franchise Association and three companies which specialize in franchise acquisition and sales. I arranged a representative, Doug, from the largest to be available for consulting with me and Thomas once he had determined the time and place. Doug and I worked on a plan to help Thomas make the transition from Toronto to BC with the most amounts of resources available with the least amount of resources expended.

I arranged for a CMA associate to fly to Toronto after Thomas told me the BC implementation needed to be moved back because of a financial situation involving cash flow issues. My CMA assured me he could analyze the situation on the ground and see what challenges Thomas had and what suggestions he could make to Thomas He will meet with Thomas in the beginning of May.

I determined from frank discussions with Thomas that finance was not a strong suit for him and he relied on a bookkeeper to advise him on strategies, forecasting, asset management etc. I felt a freelance CFO I have as an associate with an affordable one day a month plan might give him a real sense of what the financial health of the business was and how to take his business to the next step in his plan, that of having franchises. The CFO belongs to a network of freelance CFO's who parachute into companies typically with $5-15M in sales who are lacking a CFO. Generally the CFO will start at one day a month and work up to 1 or 2 days a week if needed.

I spoke with Thomas about the CFO role and how with the CFO's help he could get a better handle on both revenue and expenses. Thomas was moving into new channels without determining their profitability. I showed him how a CFO could keep him on track weekly with management reports that could show the profitability or loss of a new service product before he 'lost his shirt' on the service. Thomas also uses the buzz words associated with a corporate structure without completely knowing the mechanics behind what he was saying. He has relied on bookkeeper, albeit a competent one for all of his financing issues. The CFO would bring a new understanding to the financial statements. With a CFO on board even part time in the beginning Thomas as feeling more comfortable with our discussions that he would alleviate many of his cash flow problems and would be able to think strategically over three years instead of month by month.

We are currently working on setting up the logistics for both men to go to Toronto.

<u>Maintain Awareness of Socio-Economic Climate</u>, <u>Analyze Organizational & Operational Procedures</u> When I first met Thomas he had no idea what the economy, political landscape, employment quality or what the competition looked like for his business in BC. He was basing his decision to expand to BC because he 'liked the mountains'. It was incumbent upon me to give him as much business statistics as I could in order for him to make a business decision rather than an emotional move to BC.

Because of my position in the business community I am asked for advice and my opinion on labor market information from Business in Vancouver (a BC business newspaper) to CTV National and CTV Alberta.

I went over his pricing standards in Toronto. While he is competitive, if not slightly lower than the others, he was 70% cheaper than the BC market. I helped him identify the significant competition in BC by region and we did a comparative analysis with each compared against his business. The parameters were based on unemployment rates, home prices in BC relative to Toronto, the demographics of each community we had targeted as well as the psychographics. I suggested he may consider raising his prices to be more at a level of the competition in BC. Since his quality was well documented in Toronto I helped him realize that he could base the business on quality service rather than price.

We used resources like Stats Can, Canadian Council on Social Development, BIV magazine, Small Business BC and reviewed the industrial development plans of several regions.

Interest rates which were still low indicated home owners could afford to have disaster remediation (e.g. mold) done via loans. Home sales were up despite an economy still not fully recovered from the market crash which indicated home inspections were required. Housing starts although stalled in the US were increasing in BC. The certification of home inspectors has also taken off in BC indicating a higher standard of inspection meaning more problems would be found by fully trained inspectors. The low interest rates also allowed more people to move up in their home acquisition. First home buyers were not able to enter the market but those with homes could easily purchase up.

Household borrowing has increased each year for the last 3 decades according to Stats Can. With the proliferation of DIY television, people are more aware of the need to protect a home from mold issues so the awareness coupled with advanced inspection techniques make the business viable from a consumer need.

I pointed out to Thomas that BC had a higher than average rate of self employment with most being men between 25-54. This was a good indicator for franchising. I helped Thomas work on the structure of each Franchise operation with several keys points in mind. Branding was important so the head office would have a strong management in terms of marketing component. Liability issues were also a vital component of the organization since there health issues were being addressed by the removal of mold or lack of in a professional manner.

The liability issues also extend to the actions of the employees in a sole proprietorship where he would be covered if each franchise were to incorporate. We worked on a plan so that each new franchise would be offered an incorporation package (value $1000) which included setup of the corporation by a lawyer and an accountant. We also included a Pre-Paid Legal package (a franchised business of legal services with a monthly fee) as part of the franchise fee for one year.

The vision of Thomas business included franchises but they would be by organization franchises with a fair number of employees and contractors. This would not be run as a 'mom and pop' operation. The use of contractors when needed also suggested that a corporation would be the safest route to go, again in terms of liability. Again considering the scope of each franchise I pointed out that incorporation of each one would result in higher tax savings and benefits to the franchisee.

We went over wages and although BC announced a new minimum wage it would not affect Thomas' business as most of the employees would be certified professionals.

Finally we set up a meeting with the premier real estate professional in the area. This meeting and our criteria resulted in the identification of a prime location.

<u>Assess Technical Competency</u>, <u>Assess Client's Educational Background</u> – Since Thomas as moving into a different market it was important to determine if he and his employees met existing BC standards of competency in his industry.

We went over his technical skills as far as mold remediation. Thomas is a qualified mold expert certified through these accrediting organizations:

IICRC (Institute of Inspection Cleaning and Restoration Certification)

IIT (Institute of Infrared Thermography)

MBL (Mold and Bacteria Consulting Laboratories)

In our meetings we talked about the need for high standards for the franchise, keeping quality paramount over pricing as a determinant. Thomas and I determined that each franchise owner had to have the same designations as Thomas would insist on this and would pay for the training of the owner plus key employees.

Thomas began the business after a health issue hospitalized him because of mold in a home. He had first hand knowledge of the need for credentials, professionalism and thoroughness when it came to the practice of his business. Thomas as required by law to complete only the IICR Certification (above) but as he became more involved in the process he realized if he was to be the best in his field in Toronto, education would be a major part of his life. He continued his education with the Mold and Bacteria Laboratories.

I pointed out that new techniques must be coming along all the time to which he told me about his certification in Infrared Thermography so he could see invisible mold with a hand held device. He told me that the latest technique to kill mold was with a dry ice spray using a special device he had purchased this year. He claimed it was the only machine in operation in Toronto.

Thomas was very adamant that his employees would grow with the company as long as they had a keen interest in education. We setup a plan that employees would have their certification paid for by Thomas and that these courses could be done on company time.

Thomas and I devised a procedures manual outlining every aspect of the cleaning process from the time they arrived at the customer's home until they left. This included not only the normal cleaning procedures outlined in their certification but customer service, procedural issues with respect to arriving and leaving including greeting the customer and explaining the process that was going to be undertaken to alleviate customer anxiety. Thomas setup training and manuals for each type of cleaning operation and training sessions were regularly scheduled with 'tune-up' sessions at lunchtimes once a month. Staff who attended was given in-house certificates for the training and their lunch was provided for the tune-up sessions.

This entire package implemented at head office was the cornerstone for his service model that would differentiate Thomas and his well trained technicians from the competition.

Obviously, Thomas' business required several onsite competencies to be a leader in the field. When we analyzed his office technology he was equally impressive. I worked with Thomas to further and/or redeveloped policies, procedures and systems that are now very clear and concise. Every one of his systems now has a step by step process on how to perform each job within the company. All systems have pictures and screen shots which ensure company technicians follow step by step directions and perform their work professionally, consistently and in a world class manner.

I suggested we look into the use of hi–end CRM software to manage his customers. The program he purchased works well in Toronto. The use of the same software was incorporated in our plan for BC.

We worked on tools to make the inspection process better. Utilizing iPad with cameras special problems onsite can be diagnosed from Head office.

I suggested that we set up a communication protocol including iPhones, GPS, and Skype as components of the plan to enhance the consumer experience while giving the technicians a step ahead of the local competition.

Assist Client in Location Planning

Thomas does not know BC at all yet knew he wanted to expand here from Toronto. I assured him that between my colleagues at Franchise Link, Thomas and I could develop a plan to move ahead. He wanted to move directly via franchise into BC but after discussions I helped him realize that a more prudent method would be to setup a small 'on the ground' operation run and owned by the Toronto company to develop the market with a more solid foothold directly in touch with the market.

Thomas and I defined the territories in BC to scope out. These included the Island, metro Vancouver, Kootenays and Okanagan. I helped Thomas identify that Maple Ridge was a smaller yet central location for a new operation to begin. Out of the public eye so to speak yet within an hour of Vancouver; Maple Ridge could be suitable for a proving ground operation.

I worked with him to identify specifications on the size of property he needed the amount of his budget, showed him demographics of several areas and gave him a detailed analysis of the local labour market in BC and Maple Ridge specifically. I helped him devise a plan to lease space, vehicles, signage and which had a rental property included to assist him moving a senior person from Toronto to manage the operation.

Outcomes

I was pleased to be able to set up a very positive relationship with a man who had management issues, meaning he did not take advice easily, resulting in a very intense personal/business relationship

I assisted Thomas in making a decision to move into BC one based on solid business stats, analysis with the help of other professionals

I identified an area of counseling, HR management which resulted in a clear policy with a new staffer in charge of the hiring and administration of new employees

A location was identified through considerable market research in the main business area of Maple Ridge, BC which met the client's budget and visibility needs

After assessing the technological competencies of the organization much was added to make the employees not only more qualified but more after to communicate and have faster access to specialized resources.

To handle several financial issues and to provide the best service to the client I introduced Thomas to a qualified CFO consultant and a CMA, both of whom are in my sphere of influence and both of whom have been in contact with Thomas with plans in place to make personal contact in Toronto on the near future. Thomas was able to see how qualified senior professional staff would be an asset not a liability to his operation.

I was able to identify Thomas learning methods and effectively tune into these. He saw a great deal of sense in being more balanced when dealing with business issues. Hopefully the businessman will be more tuned into the man as he sees how it works with his business.

By assessing Thomas' educational background and his rationale for exceeding requirements we were able to develop systems which will increase his employees and franchisees understanding too.

We identified the best business structure for Thomas, that being corporations for the franchise owners. Going from Sole proprietors to corporations was a big step in the development of a world class operation in his mind

Made in the USA
Charleston, SC
20 March 2014